W9-AEZ-939

Current
CONTROVERSIES

Conserving
the Environment

Other books in the Current Controversies series

Montante Family Library
D'Youville College

Conserving
the Environment

John Woodward and Jennifer Skancke, Book Editors

GREENHAVEN PRESS

An imprint of Thomson Gale, a part of The Thomson Corporation

Detroit • New York • San Francisco • San Diego • New Haven, Conn.
Waterville, Maine • London • Munich

Bonnie Szumski, *Publisher*
Helen Cothran, *Managing Editor*

© 2006 Thomson Gale, a part of The Thomson Corporation.

Thomson and Star Logo are trademarks and Gale and Greenhaven Press are registered trademarks used herein under license.

For more information, contact:
Greenhaven Press
27500 Drake Rd.
Farmington Hills, MI 48331-3535
Or you can visit our Internet site at http://www.gale.com

ALL RIGHTS RESERVED
No part of this work covered by the copyright hereon may be reproduced or used in any form or by any means—graphic, electronic, or mechanical, including photocopying, recording, taping, Web distribution, or information storage retrieval systems—without the written permission of the publisher.

Articles in Greenhaven Press anthologies are often edited for length to meet page requirements. In addition, original titles of these works are changed to clearly present the main thesis and to explicitly indicate the author's opinion. Every effort is made to ensure that Greenhaven Press accurately reflects the original intent of the authors. Every effort has been made to trace the owners of copyrighted material.

Cover photographs reproduced by permission of © Paul A. Souders/CORBIS.

LIBRARY OF CONGRESS CATALOGING-IN-PUBLICATION DATA

Conserving the environment / John Woodward and Jennifer Skancke, book editors.
    p. cm. -- (Current controversies)
  Includes bibliographical references and index.
  0-7377-2476-5 (lib. bdg. : alk. paper) -- 0-7377-2477-3 (pbk. : alk. paper)
  1. Environmental management. 2. Environmental protection. 3. Biological diversity. I. Woodward, John 1958–. II. Skancke, Jennifer. III. Series
  GE300.C633 2007
  333.72--dc22
                                                                        2005055071

Printed in the United States of America
10 9 8 7 6 5 4 3 2 1

GE 300
.C633
2006

Contents

Chapter 1: Is the Environment in Jeopardy?

Yes: The Environment Is in Jeopardy

No: The Environment Is Not in Jeopardy

NOV 1 2006

Chapter 2: Should Global Warming Be Addressed?

Chapter 3: How Can Government Best Conserve the Environment?

Chapter 4: How Can Society Conserve the Environment?

Foreword

By definition, controversies are "discussions of questions in which opposing opinions clash" (Webster's Twentieth Century Dictionary Unabridged). Few would deny that controversies are a pervasive part of the human condition and exist on virtually every level of human enterprise. Controversies transpire between individuals and among groups, within nations and between nations. Controversies supply the grist necessary for progress by providing challenges and challengers to the status quo. They also create atmospheres where strife and warfare can flourish. A world without controversies would be a peaceful world; but it also would be, by and large, static and prosaic.

The Series' Purpose

The purpose of the Current Controversies series is to explore many of the social, political, and economic controversies dominating the national and international scenes today. Titles selected for inclusion in the series are highly focused and specific. For example, from the larger category of criminal justice, Current Controversies deals with specific topics such as police brutality, gun control, white collar crime, and others. The debates in Current Controversies also are presented in a useful, timeless fashion. Articles and book excerpts included in each title are selected if they contribute valuable, long-range ideas to the overall debate. And wherever possible, current information is enhanced with historical documents and other relevant materials. Thus, while individual titles are current in focus, every effort is made to ensure that they will not become quickly outdated. Books in the Current Controversies series will remain important resources for librarians, teachers, and students for many years.

In addition to keeping the titles focused and specific, great care is taken in the editorial format of each book in the series.

Book introductions and chapter prefaces are offered to provide background material for readers. Chapters are organized around several key questions that are answered with diverse opinions representing all points on the political spectrum. Materials in each chapter include opinions in which authors clearly disagree as well as alternative opinions in which authors may agree on a broader issue but disagree on the possible solutions. In this way, the content of each volume in Current Controversies mirrors the mosaic of opinions encountered in society. Readers will quickly realize that there are many viable answers to these complex issues. By questioning each author's conclusions, students and casual readers can begin to develop the critical thinking skills so important to evaluating opinionated material.

Current Controversies is also ideal for controlled research. Each anthology in the series is composed of primary sources taken from a wide gamut of informational categories including periodicals, newspapers, books, United States and foreign government documents, and the publications of private and public organizations. Readers will find factual support for reports, debates, and research papers covering all areas of important issues. In addition, an annotated table of contents, an index, a book and periodical bibliography, and a list of organizations to contact are included in each book to expedite further research.

Perhaps more than ever before in history, people are confronted with diverse and contradictory information. During the Persian Gulf War, for example, the public was not only treated to minute-to-minute coverage of the war, it was also inundated with critiques of the coverage and countless analyses of the factors motivating U.S. involvement. Being able to sort through the plethora of opinions accompanying today's major issues, and to draw one's own conclusions, can be a complicated and frustrating struggle. It is the editors' hope that Current Controversies will help readers with this struggle.

Introduction

| "The debate about alternative uses of wildlife refuges is fundamentally about the meaning of conservation—whether the environment is to be conserved for human use or for its own sake."

Ever since the creation of the first national wildlife preserve, Americans have debated whether alternative uses of these lands—including hunting, trapping, oil and gas exploration, and timber harvesting,—are compatible with the original mission of the refuge system. The debate about alternative uses of wildlife refuges is fundamentally about the meaning of conservation—whether the environment is to be conserved for human use or for its own sake.

From the time they first set foot on North America, the first European settlers saw the land and its plants and animals largely as resources to exploit. Over time, however, conservation advocacy groups such as the Audubon Society helped convince the public that at least some regions should be conserved and protected, and that some species of birds and animals were in danger of disappearing. As Rachel Carson, author of the landmark environmental book *Silent Spring*, put it, "Wild creatures, like men, must have a place to live."

In 1903 it was brought to President Theodore Roosevelt's attention that the pelicans and egrets on the rookery at Pelican Island, Florida, were being slaughtered for their feathers, which were used to adorn women's hats. As a result, he signed an executive order declaring the tiny island on the Indian River to be "a preserve and breeding ground for native birds." He later wrote in his autobiography that he intended to "preserve from destruction beautiful and wonderful wild creatures whose existence was threatened by greed and wantonness." The first national wildlife refuge had been created with the stroke of his pen.

Although Roosevelt was an avid hunter and fisherman, he envisioned refuges as safe harbors for the animals that lived there. Roosevelt would go on to designate fifty more refuges, in addition to 150 national forests, five national parks, and eighteen national monuments. Today there are 540 wildlife refuges encompassing 95 million acres and inhabited by seven hundred species of birds and an equal number of other vertebrate species. The American National Wildlife Refuge (NWR) system is the most comprehensive system of land dedicated to wildlife preservation in the world, and it is widely praised. The vast majority of Americans support the notion of setting aside some public lands for wildlife.

In the century since Roosevelt initiated the wildlife refuge system, however, alternative uses of refuge land have increased dramatically. It surprises most people to learn that less than 2 percent of the refuges in the NWR system are closed to the public. In fact, 311 refuges allow hunting, 280 allow trapping, and 155 either are being or have been used for oil and gas exploration. All of these uses of the refuges are controversial.

Hunting and conservation advocacy organizations such as Ducks Unlimited and Safari Club International argue that their efforts to preserve wetlands and boost some wildlife populations benefit the environment. They believe that hunting is a legitimate and beneficial use of wildlife refuges. According to Ducks Unlimited executive vice president Don Young, "Hunting is not the threat to North America's wildlife populations. Habitat loss is the primary threat."

Others believe that allowing hunting and trapping in refuges defeats the purpose of the system. "It is clear that the U.S. Fish and Wildlife Service has lost sight of the meaning of 'refuge' and the original purpose of the National Wildlife Refuge System," says Camilla Fox, director of wildlife programs for the Animal Protection Institute. "That wildlife can be trapped and killed in cruel leghold traps and snares for their fur on National Wildlife Refuges is a contradiction in terms and ethics," Fox asserts.

Recently there has been much debate about allowing oil exploration in the Arctic National Wildlife Refuge (ANWR). Advocates claim that vital energy resources can be extracted without disturbing the resident wildlife. According to U.S. senator Jim Bunning, "Recent advances in technology enable us to successfully extract oil in ANWR in an environmentally sensitive way. The old stereotypes of dirty oil drilling just don't apply anymore." Opponents, however, argue that environmental damage as a result of oil exploration is inevitable. "It is foolish to say oil development and a wildlife refuge can coexist," says U.S. senator Maria Cantwell.

The arguments over alternative uses of wildlife refuges are part of a broader debate about the meaning and purpose of conservation itself. The viewpoints in *Current Controversies: Conserving the Environment* examine several of the major controversies surrounding conservation early in the twenty-first century.

CHAPTER 1

Is the Environment in Jeopardy?

Chapter Preface

From the time of the first European exploration of North America, most Americans have generally considered the environment to be an unlimited resource meant to be exploited. Although there have long been American conservationists, they were often viewed as eccentrics. The modern environmental movement, which polls indicate is supported by the vast majority of the public, is a recent phenomenon. Concern for the state of the environment entered the general public's consciousness largely as a result of one book, *Silent Spring*, and grew into a movement that a few years later resulted in the first Earth Day celebration. For many early activists, the movement's most important achievement was prompting the government to create a cabinet-level agency charged with the protection of the environment, the Environmental Protection Agency (EPA).

Rachel Carson's *Silent Spring* was published in 1962. The book was Carson's attempt to inform the public about the danger associated with the widespread use of pesticides, which she claimed were harmful to birds, animals, and humans. "Over increasingly large areas of the United States," she wrote, "spring now comes unheralded by the return of birds, and the early mornings are strangely silent where once they were filled with the beauty of bird song." Carson was an avid birdwatcher, and her primary concern was the declining population of birds at the top of the food chain, including raptors such as the bald eagle, whose eggs often broke before hatching because the shells had become brittle due to the eagles' absorption of the pesticide DDT from their prey. Most of Carson's readers, however, were more concerned about the impact of environmental pollution on human welfare. Nevertheless, *Silent Spring* is considered one of the most important inspirations for the modern environmental movement. Carson was not without her critics, however. The chemical industry attacked her for what it considered faulty science and exaggeration. Some critics today, in fact, contend that the majority of Carson's claims about pesticides—except for DDT's effects on raptor eggshells—have largely been disproved. But the broader idea took root in the public's mind that the natural environment, especially the air and water, had become dangerously polluted, and that something had to be done about it. This concern reached critical mass with the establishment of Earth Day.

The driving force behind Earth Day was Senator Gaylord Nelson, whose objective, he said, was "to show the political leadership of the nation that there was broad and deep support for the environmental movement." On April 22, 1970, Earth Day celebrations occurred across the United States. It is estimated that Earth Day activities were held at two thousand colleges and universities and ten thousand high schools and grade schools. The more than 20 million people who participated demonstrated to politicians of both parties that concern about the state of the environment was firmly in the mainstream of popular thought. Earth Day has been observed annually by millions of Americans for more than three decades.

The momentum begun on April 22, 1970, led to action less than three months later. On July 9, President Richard Nixon submitted to Congress a governmental reorganization plan that included the creation of the Environmental Protection Agency, which opened its doors for business on December 2. In his message to Congress, Nixon wrote: "As concern with the condition of our physical environment has intensified. . .it has become increasingly clear that only by reorganizing our Federal efforts can we. . .effectively ensure the protection, development, and enhancement of the total environment." The creation of the EPA represented an official, bipartisan acknowledgment that threats to the environment were real and that mitigating them was a responsibility of the government. On June 14, 1972, the use of DDT was outlawed in the United States by the EPA. Rachel Carson did not live to witness this action, however; she had died in 1964.

More than three decades after the creation of the environmental watchdog agency, the authors of the viewpoints in this chapter take part in the still lively debate about the state of the environment.

An Environmental Crisis Exists

Environment Earth

About the author: Environment Earth is a nonprofit educational resource organization dedicated to increasing public appreciation of the environment and spreading awareness of environmental issues.

It is easy in daily life to overlook the fact that the earth's resources, as vast as they may seem, are limited. Although most environmental threats are well known, it is worth reviewing the most important ways that people influence the earth's atmosphere and climate.

Fossil Fuels

The burning of fossil fuels such as gasoline, oil, and coal causes particles contained in the smoke and fumes to rise into the atmosphere, where they remain suspended for many years. Carbon dioxide and other gases are also released into the atmosphere. Scientists are concerned about the long-term effect of these pollutants on the world's climate. One well-documented effect is global warming—a steady increase in temperatures that could cause widespread drought, famine, and, as the glaciers melt, flooding of the world's major population centers.

The atmosphere is becoming thinner, allowing more radiation from the sun to reach the ground.

The toxic chemicals released by the burning of fossil fuels also mix with water in the air and fall back to earth as acid

Environment Earth, "Environment Basics," www.environment-earth.com, 2003. Copyright © 2003 by Dennis L. Foster. Reproduced by permission.

rain. This type of precipitation corrodes buildings and vehicles and alters the composition of lakes and streams, killing fish, birds, and other wildlife.

The atmosphere is becoming thinner, allowing more radiation from the sun to reach the ground. Most of the oxygen in the atmosphere is produced by the tropical rain forests. But the development of large-scale cattle-raising, mining, farming, and logging operations in many countries of the world has led to the destruction of vast sections of the rain forests. As a result, the atmosphere is becoming thinner, allowing more radiation from the sun to reach the ground.

Destruction of the Ozone Layer

Exposure to ultraviolet radiation from the sun is a major cause of skin cancer, including a usually fatal form of melanoma. Ultraviolet rays also damage grain, vegetable, and fruit crops. Normally, the upper layer of the earth's atmosphere, the ozone, deflects much of the sun's ultraviolet radiation. When NASA [National Aeronautics and Space Administration] scientists gathered data about the ozone from a satellite, they discovered that the ozone layer was thinner than it was ten years earlier. The satellite also discovered a hole in the ozone layer that allows ultraviolet radiation to penetrate the atmosphere. Chemical propellants used in aerosol cans, the manufacture of styrofoam products, test explosions of nuclear weapons, and high-altitude aircraft flights are all thought to contribute to the destruction of the ozone layer.

Automobile exhaust and other chemical fumes interact with ultraviolet radiation to form smog. In cities with high concentrations of smog, a disproportionate number of people die of lung cancer. Smog also destroys crops and other plant life.

Polluted Water

The hydrosphere is not immune to the effects of pollution. Industrial wastes dumped into rivers, streams, and lakes poison wildlife and contaminate drinking water. Pesticides and other chemicals used in agriculture pollute the soil and seep into the groundwater.

In the oceans, accidents involving oil tankers and offshore drilling platforms destroy thousands of fish, birds, and marine mammals. Many more thousands of dolphins, turtles, and other ocean creatures are routinely killed when they become entangled in huge drift nets strung by fishing fleets. Many species may soon become extinct as a direct result of these abuses, altering the balance of life in the oceans.

Accidents involving oil tankers and offshore drilling platforms destroy thousands of fish, birds, and marine mammals.

When a rain forest is destroyed, large amounts of carbon dioxide are released into the atmosphere by the decaying vegetation. About a third of the carbon dioxide that pollutes the upper atmosphere is caused by the destruction of rain forests.

Furthermore, at the current deforestation rate, a plant and animal species becomes extinct at the rate of one species per hour.

Reclaiming the Environment

Reclaiming the environment and reversing the destruction of the earth's atmosphere, rain forests, and water quality requires a concentrated effort of governments, companies, communities, and individuals. The development of fuels that result in lower levels of air pollution is one positive step toward reclaiming the atmosphere. Conserving energy is the most immediate way to reduce pollution from carbon dioxide. If power plants burn less coal and other fossil fuels, the level of carbon dioxide in the atmosphere will decline. Other important steps include halting the destruction of rain forests, reducing the output of industrial wastes, and recycling paper, glass, and metals used in the manufacture of packaging materials.

Federal, state, and local governments have enacted various regulations and, in some cases, imposed fines to stop industrialists and farmers from polluting the soil and water. At the federal level, the Environmental Protection Agency (EPA) is responsible for conducting research into air, water, and land pollution and developing standards and methods for reducing the threat to the environment.

The EPA classifies environmental problems by the level of risk, as follows:

- *High risk*: Habitat destruction; global warming; ozone layer depletion; species extinction

- *Medium risk*: Herbicides and pesticides; surface water pollution; airborne toxic substances

- *Low risk*: Oil spills; radioactive materials; groundwater pollution

- *Human health risks*: Air pollution; drinking water pollution; exposure to chemicals

The Extinction of Plants and Animals Is a Serious Problem

Mark Buchanan

About the author: Mark Buchanan is the author of Small World: Uncovering Nature's Hidden Networks.

An international team of marine ecologists recently completed an exhaustive historical study of coastal ecosystems, ranging from coral reefs and tropical seagrass beds to river estuaries and continental shelves. Their findings were disturbing. In every case, fish numbers had declined precipitously with the onset of modern methods of industrial fishing. As the researchers concluded: "Everywhere, the magnitude of losses was enormous in terms of biomass and abundance of large animals that are now effectively absent."

The situation has become especially critical in the past few decades. Stocks of Atlantic cod have reached historic lows, while haddock and other species have been declared commercially extinct. Thriving food webs that were stable for millions of years have in the past 20 been radically altered, and almost three quarters of the world's commercially important marine fish stocks are now fully fished, overexploited or depleted.

This is just one illustration of the trouble facing the global ecosystem. Biologists estimate that the rate of species extinction worldwide is at least a thousand times greater now than it was before human beings walked the earth, and that one-quarter of all species could be obliterated in 50 years.

But does it really matter to us? The political scientist Bjorn Lomborg, in *The Skeptical Environmentalist,* has argued that much of what environmentalists have said is overstated—that fears of ecosystem collapse are irrational and largely the result

Mark Buchanan, "The Extinction of Species and Why it Matters More than You Think," *New Statesman*, vol. 131, July 8, 2002, p. 30. Copyright © 2002 by New Statesman, Ltd. Reproduced by permission.

of scare tactics. On a strict cost-benefit analysis, he says, the consequences of species extinction, like those of global warming, are not serious enough to warrant the expense of trying to stop them. We are better off trying to adapt—by seeking other sources of fish to eat, for example. And many others think the extinction of species is of interest and concern only to nature lovers.

Living Networks

Any ecosystem . . . is a staggeringly complex network in which many species interact with one another in delicate and all but unfathomable patterns. Any ecosystem, however, is a staggeringly complex network in which many species interact with one another in delicate and all but unfathomable patterns. Indeed, it is our inability to understand how these living networks hang together—and consequently, how they might fall apart—that has seriously undermined efforts to assess the vulnerability of the global ecosystem. But in the past few years, researchers have discovered that ecological networks are not unique in their complexity. In their basic architecture and pattern of assembly, ecosystems turn out to be in many ways identical to other complex networks such as the internet, and even to our webs of social acquaintances.

Any ecosystem . . . is a staggeringly complex network in which many species interact with one another in delicate and all but unfathomable patterns.

What emerges from this new science is anything but reassuring. The biological world turns out to be a remarkably small one, with the predator-prey links between species arranged in such a way that no species is more than a handful of steps away from any other. More than anyone suspected, the global ecosystem is an intimately connected whole, and we should indeed be very worried about what we are doing to it.

Most of us have run into a friend of a friend far away from home and felt that the world is somehow smaller than we thought. We usually put such encounters down to coincidence even though they happen with disconcerting frequency. Recent scientific work suggests that this "small world" phenomenon is by no means limited to social relations.

In the social setting, the "small world" experience is closely linked to the notion of "six degrees of separation"—the idea that each of us is linked to everyone else on the planet by a chain of no more than six intermediary acquaintances. Amazingly, this seems to be roughly true. In the 1960s, the American social psychologist Stanley Milgram sent letters to random people living in Nebraska and Kansas, asking each to forward the letter to a stockbroker friend of his living in Boston. He stipulated that they were to send the letter only to someone they knew personally and whom they thought might be socially "closer" to this man. Even though the US then had a population of around 200 million, most of the letters made it to the stockbroker in just five or six mailings.

The Interconnected World

Researchers have found similarly small worlds in many other settings. The worldwide web is a network of more than one billion sites connected by hypertext links. Take two sites at random, and it needs only about 19 clicks to get from one to the other. Other studies have come upon a similar architecture in the layout of the world's electrical power grids, in the patterns of neural connections in the mammalian brain, and in the web of chemical reactions within the living cell. The world's ecosystems—or more precisely, the food webs that underlie them—appear to share this "small world" character.

The tapestry of life is made of a truly dense cloth. How many species-to-species links does it take to link any two organisms in some chain of cause and effect? In the ecological setting, two species are linked if one feeds upon the other, be

A commercial logger cuts down a tree in the rainforest of Gabon, Africa. © Gallo Images/ CORBIS

it a fox eating a rabbit or a beetle munching an oak leaf. Last year [2001], a Spanish physicist, Ricard Sole, and an ecologist, Jose Montoya, studied Silwood Park, an ecosystem in the UK [United Kingdom] for which researchers know the fairly complete food web. They found the number of degrees of separation to be only two or three. The tapestry of life is made of a truly dense cloth.

The tapestry of life is made of a truly dense cloth.

Silwood Park does not represent the global ecosystem; it is certainly more than two steps from a woodpecker in Illinois to a shrimp in the South China Sea. Even so, whales and many species of fish populate the oceans as a whole, and numerous birds migrate between the continents. Bacteria, algae, tiny spiders and other creatures fly round the world in storm systems. Those organisms provide links that tie the biological world together. For the global ecosystem, the number of degrees of separation may not be two, but it is probably not much higher than ten.

This discovery is not comforting. It suggests that the extinction of one species will affect not only everything that the species eats, competes with, or is eaten by, but will send out fingers of influence which, in a few steps, will reach most other species in the entire system. It suggests that any belief in our capacity to control the effects of ecological destruction is badly misplaced. That lesson becomes clearer as one delves more closely into the small-world phenomenon and into exactly how large networks—such as the human social network—can be so remarkably small.

Strong and Weak Ties

As first suggested by the American sociologist Mark Granovetter in the 1970s, the answer can be seen by making a distinction between "strong" and "weak" social ties. Strong ties bind us to family members and good friends, or to colleagues at work. These links form the threads of a dense fabric of social structure, and are socially most important to us. But these are not the ties that make for a small world.

Each of us also has "weak" links to people we see rarely, or may never see again. Think of some of your friends from the past—long-lost college mates, say. Or someone you met when travelling. Perhaps you went to Japan and briefly made friends with a fellow tourist from Australia. Your links to this person, or to those friends now out of touch, are weak social links.

What makes them especially important is that they connect you to people who otherwise belong to quite distinct social spheres. Your link to the Australian tourist, for example, establishes a social bridge that connects you in just two steps to every person this man knows. Not only that, but this single link connects each of your local acquaintances, in London, say, to every one of his local acquaintances in Australia. In this way, weak links act like short cuts through the social world.

Mathematics backs up this insight. In 1998, in a paper published in *Nature,* two mathematicians from Cornell University showed that the effect of weak ties in a social network really does explain six degrees of separation. In a large network—even one of six billion people—just a few weak links running between people from distant places will indeed make for an extremely small world, with every pair of persons linked by a short chain of intermediaries.

The small-world character of the world's ecosystems can be traced to similarly weak links—that is, to links between species that interact only occasionally. Perhaps just one bird in an English wood migrates long distances, and, en route, settles briefly in southern Spain. This is enough to link the organisms of these two food webs together by short chains of cause and effect.

Maintaining Ecosystem Stability

But ecologists are beginning to suspect that weak links within food webs also play an important role in maintaining ecosystem stability. Their argument is subtle, but important, as it could help us to protect the world's food webs from disintegration.

If a predator eats just one other species, it will do so frequently, having no other options. Consequently, the link between these species will be strong. Conversely, if a predator feeds upon 15 different prey, it may eat each species only occasionally. It will then have relatively weak links with these species.

The loss of a strong link within a food web will be destabilising, tending to stir up large and dangerous fluctuations in species numbers.

Suppose that, after a climate change or some human intrusion, the numbers of a predator's favourite prey have been severely depleted. What will happen? If this particular predator feeds on only this one prey—if they share a strong link, that is—then the predator must continue to seek that prey even though its numbers are vanishing, driving this species even closer to extinction. When this happens, the population of predators may then fall precipitously as well. As a paper in *Nature* pointed out a few years ago, this should be a general tendency: the loss of a strong link within a food web will be destabilising, tending to stir up large and dangerous fluctuations in species numbers.

The loss of a strong link within a food web will be desta-bilising, tending to stir up large and dangerous fluctua-tions in species numbers.

But weaker links can save the day. Consider a predator with 15 different prey. If the numbers of one of these species become very low, for whatever reason, the natural response of the predator is to shift its attention to another species that is more numerous and easier to catch. As a result, the predator would continue to find food, while the prey in danger of extinction could revive its numbers. In this way, weak links between species not only make for a small ecological world but also act as natural pressure valves, playing a central role in guaranteeing the health of an ecosystem.

Superconnected Species

You might expect that all species would have roughly the same number of links with other species. Not so. Nature doesn't dole the links out equitably. Studies in Silwood Park and elsewhere reveal that a few species always play the role of superconnected hubs: they "own a high fraction of the links in the food web, far and away more than the average species."

By simple logic, most of these links will be weak links. So these hub species provide the network with an ability to redistribute stress and prevent one species from wiping out another by uncontrolled predation or competition. And that explains why we should be so worried about extinctions.

Half the tropical forests, where two-thirds of all species find their habitat, have now been logged or burned to clear land for human development, with another one million square kilometres disappearing every five to ten years. If healthy ecosystems are small worlds characterised by a few hub species, with a preponderance of weak links providing their stability, then the global depletion of species numbers is truly alarming. As species continue to disappear, the remaining species will necessarily be linked more strongly—if only by simple arithmetic. If some predator preys on only six species where before it preyed upon ten, its links with the six will be stronger, and ecosystem stability can only suffer. As one ecologist, Kevin McCann, argues, the lesson is that, if we wish to preserve an ecosystem, or any species within it, we had best proceed "as if each species is sacred".

Linchpins of the Living World

What's more, the consequences of removing just one of the "superconnected" species can be dramatic, as a huge number of weak stabilising links would go with it. Ecologists have long talked about "keystone" species, crucial organisms whose removal might bring the web of life tumbling down like a house of cards. A recent study has demonstrated just how crucial their preservation may be.

Suppose you begin removing species from an ecosystem. Slowly but surely, the food web should fall apart. But how? First the good news. Sole and Montoya have used a computer to mimic the loss of species from a food web and have found that real communities stand up relatively well when the species to be removed are selected at random. Now the bad news. Suppose instead that the most highly connected species get knocked out first. In this case, ecological disaster ensues quickly. Removing even 20 per cent of the most highly connected species fragments the web almost entirely, splintering it into many tiny pieces. As the web falls apart, the disintegration triggers numerous secondary extinctions as some species lose all their connections to others and become totally isolated.

The obvious answer is to take special care to preserve the highly connected "hub" species. But it is not easy to predict which species will be the hubs for any particular food web. In the past, ecologists have suspected that the hubs would tend to be large predators, but this does not seem to be true. Sole and Montoya found that they were often inconspicuous organisms in the middle of the food chain, or were sometimes basic plants at the very bottom.

Most species now going extinct are ants, beetles and other kinds of insect. Some take comfort in this, but they are wrong to do so. These species may well be linchpins of the living fabric.

What Sole and Montoya achieved on their computer, human activity is achieving, in reality—the methodical dismantling of the world's ecosystems. The leaders of many governments and large corporations find it convenient to suppose that worries about the ecosystem are overstated, and anyway, that it would be demented to carry out reforms that are not politically popular. But we are disassembling the web of life that supports our existence, with little understanding of what we are doing. That is truly demented.

Human Overpopulation Harms the Environment

Roger A. Rosenblatt

About the author: Roger A. Rosenblatt is a professor of family medicine at the University of Washington School of Medicine in Seattle, Washington.

The patient is an elderly woman, beloved in her community, who comes to your office with a list of serious problems. She has night sweats and fevers that have been getting worse for the last few years. She has difficulty breathing and on examination seems to have suffered from aspiration pneumonia. She has alopecia, having lost her hair in a patchy distribution. Her normal gastrointestinal flora has been invaded by a few noxious species, and she has persistent diarrhea. Her skin is marked by an extensive dermatitis: it is fissured, inflamed, gouged, scraped, denuded, and cracking in many places. These excoriations are caused by a small but extremely industrious organism whose numbers have grown exponentially during the last few years, displacing and even eliminating other organisms that used to be widely distributed on the skin of our patient.

Differential Diagnosis: Global Environmental Change

The patient, of course, is Earth. Each symptom reflects one of a series of environmental perturbations that are threatening the homeostasis of the marvelous planet we call home. It is useful to consider each of these symptoms individually and to examine the way they interact to spawn a disease complex that demands our urgent attention as physicians, humans, and members of a biological community.

Roger A. Rosenblatt, "Ecological Change and the Future of the Human Species," *Annals of Family Medicine*, vol. 3, March/April 2005, pp. 173–76. Copyrigth © 2005 by *Annals of Family Medicine*. Reproduced by permission.

Night Sweats and Fevers: Global Warming

Human production of greenhouse gases—in particular carbon dioxide, methane, and the chlorofluorocarbonsa—has led to increases in Earth's surface temperature. Global warming is a reality, and the inevitable rise in carbon dioxide alone will lead to further increases in mean global temperature of 2°F to 10°F this century. The problem is even more acute in the growing number of mega-cities in which the human population increasingly clusters. These population centers become heat islands that are 7°F to 10°F hotter than the surrounding countryside.

The consequences of global warming will have profound effects on Earth and its inhabitants. Rising sea levels will cause flooding of low-lying islands and coastal communities. Heat itself causes devastating heat waves. The 2003 summer heat wave in France killed 10 times more people than died from severe acute respiratory syndrome (SARS) worldwide between 2002 and 2004. This climate change is very likely to increase the range of insect vectors that carry a number of virulent diseases, including malaria, dengue fever, West Nile virus, and encephalitis.

The greatest culprit is the burning of fossil fuels to run our cars, factories, and the air conditioners with which we attempt to survive the heat waves that cause these global night sweats. As the developing world strives to match the lifestyles of the Western world, the problem will accelerate.

Respiratory Distress: Poor Air Quality

We take air for granted—usually. Breathe in, breathe out, thousands of times a day, millions of times in a lifetime. But breathing can be misery, and for growing numbers of people, respiration is a constant grim challenge.

Asthma is among the most common afflictions, and both the prevalence and the severity of this disease are increasing. Despite the development of powerful new treatments for asthma, wheezing kids fill our urban emergency departments. Epidemics of asthma sweep through urban communities with the rapidity and morbidity of influenza, but immunizations cannot protect the vulnerable.

Although we do not fully understand all the elements of the respiratory disease epidemic that has swept the world during the last few decades, one factor is contaminated air. The Clean Air Act of 1970 led to some improvements in air quality in the United States, but progress has not been uniform, and the administration of George W. Bush has attempted to weaken existing environmental protections. Global warming exacerbates the impact of air pollution; ozone levels rise in tandem with air temperature, and ozone is one of the more virulent causes of air pollution.

As we spew pollutants into the great common air sheds upon which we depend, everybody inhales equal opportunity toxins. Deteriorating air is further paralleled in polluted water, another rate-limiting substance upon which not only humans, but all species, depend.

Alopecia: Deforestation

Our patient's alopecia is mirrored in the deforestation of our globe. In the Amazon, forests are burned to allow crops to be planted, even though the thin soil is depleted after one or two crop rotations. In Nepal and Central America, growing rural populations walk farther each day from their villages to cut firewood from the dwindling forests. In Africa, drought and global warming feed the expanding deserts. In the 1990s alone, human activities led to the loss of more than 500,000 square miles of forests.

The story of Easter Island illustrates how much our well-being is tied to the trees that support our world in more than a metaphoric way. Polynesians colonized the island in the fifth century, attracted in part by existing forests that seemed to offer an inexhaustible supply of wood to build houses, sea-going canoes, and the log rollers that allowed them to construct the fantastic stone monuments for which the island is famous. The entire civilization collapsed several generations later largely because the trees were harvested unsustainably, leading to mass famine when the Easter Islanders could not replace the canoes upon which their fishery depended. The Polynesians who cut the trees did not imagine the catastrophic consequences of deforestation for their once-thriving civilization. Can we?

The rapid growth in human population . . . has transformed Earth and altered the basic geochemical cycles upon which life depends.

Diarrhea: Loss of Biodiversity

Just as our gastrointestinal tracts need a spectrum of normal bacteria for healthy functioning, our globe benefits from the amazing diversity of life. Evolution is beginning to run in reverse. Species that inhabited Earth long before humans emerged are being eradicated by mass extinctions. As we crowd out other species by our manipulation of the globe, we are impoverished by the loss of species that provide us with food, oxygen, medicine, and aesthetic enjoyment.

Species extinction is invisible to most of us. The planetary system seems so robust that it seems unlikely that we could be threatened by the loss of a few bugs or birds that few of us have heard of. The whole intricate complex is quite fragile, however, and our genomic sciences are no substitute for the immense archive of DNA that is the legacy of billions of years of evolution. Which is the keystone species whose loss will lead to the collapse of the whole edifice?

Dermatitis: Overpopulation

The rapid growth in human population . . . has transformed

Earth and altered the basic geochemical cycles upon which life depends. The world's population has grown from fewer than 100 million people 3,000 years ago to 6.3 billion people today, with two thirds of the increase in the last 50 years. By the year 2050 the world population is projected to range from 7.4 billion to 10.6 billion people. The rapid growth in human population, and the increased resource consumption generated both by the sheer number of humans and the rapid pace of development has transformed Earth and altered the basic geochemical cycles upon which life depends.

The population burden of humans affects our own species as well as those with whom we share the globe. Although it may seem demeaning to think of the human species as a form of lice, our collective impact on the surface of the globe is even greater than that of scabies on the skin of our hapless patient. The human population has not only affected Earth's crust and the thin organic layer that covers it, but human activities have also depleted and polluted ground water, altered the chemistry of the atmosphere, and changed the genetic composition of much of the plant life growing on the planet. The population burden of humans affects our own species as well as those with whom we share the globe.

The population burden of humans affects our own species as well as those with whom we share the globe.

Overpopulation not only drives environmental degradation but can contribute to poverty, social polarization, and large-scale human migration. Stabilization of Earth's human population is an important first step in any attempt to restore equilibrium to our natural and social processes.

The Medical Response: What Can We Do?

As Paul Ehrlich has pointed out, the human species is superb at countering acute crises and dismal at addressing slow-moving threats. We have mobilized a rapid and effective global response to the threats represented by bioterrorism and SARS, but we seem paralyzed in the face of the much slower collapse of the ecosystem on which all depend.

Despair is unacceptable—the situation is much too serious for acquiescence. There are some concrete steps that we as citizens and health professionals can take.

Expand Your Perspective

Just as we have gone beyond the purely biological in medicine to incorporate both the psychological and the social, so can we realize that there is an ecological dimension to much of what we do. We are related to all the other species carrying shards of billion-year-old DNA in their cells, and we share a common existence and a common fate. By increasing our awareness of the connectedness of all living organisms, we can use our talents as healers to restore the vitality of the web of life.

Help Prevent Unwanted Pregnancies

Probably the most important thing we can do as a physician is to help people control their own fertility. The most logical place to begin for those of us in family medicine would be in the area of family planning, an area in which we already have the clinical responsibility and the requisite skills. One of the most effective ways to stabilize population levels is to prevent unintended pregnancy.

Probably the most important thing we can do as a physician is to help people control their own fertility.

A distressingly large proportion of pregnancies are unplanned and unwanted, often disrupting and impoverishing the families where they occur. Simply by reducing the number of unintended pregnancies, we could achieve a dramatic reduction in the overall birth rate, a reduction that if replicated worldwide could have a marked impact on the rate of population rise. Even though much of the problem lies outside the industrialized world, the United States has a disproportionate effect on the policies of other countries.

Encourage Sustainable Economies

We can use our influence to shape the economic activities of our own community, and change our own behavior to set an example. Economic development is critical to the social well-being of a community, but not if it destroys the resources on which it depends.

Stay Engaged with the Natural World

Life is not a pixilated image on a shimmering screen. We must immerse ourselves in the exhilarating symphony of the natural world—cherish and preserve the beauty that remains, work to repair the damage done by others, and walk gently on this Earth.

The doctor is sanctioned by society as a healer and, as such, has the opportunity to influence the conditions that promote or undermine good health. This position of privilege also carries the responsibility to use our talents and energy, not only to mend the ills of our individual patients, but to improve the milieu in which they live. It is time to acknowledge the enormous ecological issues that affect the very substrate of life itself but that lie outside the traditional boundaries of our profession. The practice of medicine cannot proceed in a vacuum, insulated from the catastrophic changes in the ecosystem upon which life depends. We have the ability to repair much of the harm we have done. Now we need the will.

Environmentalists Exaggerate Environmental Problems

Ronald Bailey

Ronald Bailey is the science correspondent for Reason, *a libertarian magazine.*

Thirty Years ago, 20 million Americans participated in the first Earth Day on April 22, 1970. Fifth Avenue in New York City was closed to automobiles as 100,000 people joined in concerts, lectures, and street theater. More than 2,000 colleges and universities across America paused their anti-war protests to rally instead against pollution and population growth. Even Congress recessed, acknowledging that the environment was now on a political par with motherhood. Since that first Earth Day, the celebrations have only gotten bigger, if somewhat less dramatic: The organizers of Earth Day 2000 . . . expect 500 million people around the globe to participate. . . .

Earth Day 1970 provoked a torrent of apocalyptic predictions. "We have about five more years at the outside to do something," ecologist Kenneth Watt declared to a Swarthmore College audience on April 19, 1970. Harvard biologist George Wald estimated that "civilization will end within 15 or 30 years unless immediate action is taken against problems facing mankind." "We are in an environmental crisis which threatens the survival of this nation, and of the world as a suitable place of human habitation," wrote Washington University biologist Barry Commoner in the Earth Day issue of the scholarly journal *Environment*. . . .

Three decades later, of course, the world hasn't come to an end; if anything, the planet's ecological future has never looked

Ronald Bailey, "Earth Day, Then and Now" *Reason*, May 2000. Copyright © 2000 by the Reason Foundation, 3415 S. Sepulveda Blvd., Suite 400, Los Angeles, CA 90034. www.reason.com.Reproduced by permission.

so promising. With half a billion people suiting up around the globe for Earth Day 2000, now is a good time to look back on the predictions made at the first Earth Day and see how they've held up and what we can learn from them. The short answer: The prophets of doom were not simply wrong, but *spectacularly* wrong.

Earth Day 1970 provoked a torrent of apocalyptic predictions.

More important, many contemporary environmental alarmists are similarly mistaken when they continue to insist that the Earth's future remains an eco-tragedy that has already entered its final act. Such doomsters not only fail to appreciate the huge environmental gains made over the past 30 years, they ignore the simple fact that increased wealth, population, and technological innovation don't degrade and destroy the environment. Rather, such developments preserve and enrich the environment. If it is impossible to predict fully the future, it is nonetheless possible to learn from the past. And the best lesson we can learn from revisiting the discourse surrounding the very first Earth Day is that passionate concern, however sincere, is no substitute for rational analysis.

The prophets of doom were not simply wrong, but spectacularly wrong.

The "Population Bomb" Theory Bombed

Imminent global famine caused by the explosion of the "population bomb" was *the* big issue on Earth Day 1970. Then—and now—the most prominent prophet of population doom was Stanford University biologist Paul Ehrlich. Dubbed "ecology's angry lobbyist" by *Life* magazine, the gloomy Ehrlich was quoted everywhere. "Population will inevitably and completely outstrip whatever small increases in food supplies we make," he confidently declared in an interview with then-radical journalist Peter Collier in the April 1970 *Mademoiselle*. "The death rate will increase until at least 100–200 million people per year will be starving to death during the next ten years.". . .

Although Ehrlich was certainly the most strident doomster, he was far from alone in his famine forecasts. "It is already too late to avoid mass starvation," declared Denis Hayes, the chief organizer for Earth Day, in the Spring 1970 issue of *The Living Wilderness*. . . .

Time has not been gentle with these prophecies. It's absolutely true that far too many people remain poor and hungry in the world—800 million people are still malnourished and nearly 1.2 billion live on less than a dollar a day—but we have not seen mass starvation around the world in the past three decades. Where we have seen famines, such as in Somalia and Ethiopia, they are invariably the result of war and political instability. Indeed, far from turning brown, the Green Revolution has never been so verdant. Food production has handily outpaced population growth and food today is cheaper and more abundant than ever before. . . .

The Pollution Mistake

Pollution was the other big issue on Earth Day 1970. Smog choked many American cities and sludge coated the banks of many rivers. People were also worried that we were poisoning the biosphere and ourselves with dangerous pesticides. DDT, which had been implicated in the decline of various bird species, including the bald eagle, the peregrine falcon, and the brown pelican, would soon be banned in the United States. Students wearing gas masks buried cars and internal combustion engines as symbols of our profligate and polluting consumer society. The Great Lakes were in bad shape and Lake Erie was officially "dead," its fish killed because oxygen supplies had been depleted by rotting algae blooms that had themselves been fed by organic pollutants from factories and municipal sewage. Pesticides draining from the land were projected to kill off the phytoplankton in the oceans, eventually stopping oxygen production.

Far from turning brown, the Green Revolution has never been so verdant.

In January 1970, *Life* reported, "Scientists have solid experimental and theoretical evidence to support . . . the following predictions: In a decade, urban dwellers will have to wear gas masks to survive air pollution . . . by 1985 air pollution will have reduced the amount of sunlight reaching earth by one half. . . ." Ecologist Kenneth Watt told *Time* that, "At the present rate of nitrogen buildup, it's only a matter of time before light will be filtered out of the atmosphere and none of our land will be usable." Barry Commoner cited a National Research Council report that had estimated "that by 1980 the oxygen demand due to municipal wastes will equal the oxygen content of the total flow of all the U.S. river systems in the summer months." Translation: Decaying organic pollutants would use up all of the oxygen in America's rivers, causing freshwater fish to suffocate.

Of course, the irrepressible Ehrlich chimed in, predicting in his *Mademoiselle* interview that "air pollution . . . is certainly going to take hundreds of thousands of lives in the next few years alone." In *Ramparts*, Ehrlich sketched a scenario in which 200,000 Americans would die in 1973 during "smog disasters" in New York and Los Angeles.

So has air pollution gotten worse? Quite the contrary. In the most recent National Air Quality Trends report, the U.S. Environmental Protection Agency—itself created three decades ago partly as a response to Earth Day celebrations—had this to say: "Since 1970, total U.S. population increased 29 percent, vehicle miles traveled increased 121 percent, and the gross domestic product (GDP) increased 104 percent. During that same period, notable reductions in air quality concentrations and emissions took place." Since 1970, ambient levels of sulfur dioxide and carbon monoxide have fallen by 75 percent, while total suspended particulates like smoke, soot, and dust have been cut by 50 percent since the 1950s.

In 1988, the particulate standard was changed to account for smaller particles. Even under this tougher standard, particulates have declined an additional 15 percent. Ambient ozone and nitrogen dioxide, prime constituents of smog, are both down by 30 percent since the 1970s. According to the EPA, the total number of days with air pollution alerts dropped 56 percent in Southern California and 66 percent in the remaining major cities in the United States between 1988 and 1997. Since at least the early 1990s, residents of infamously smogged-in Los Angeles have been able to see that their city is surrounded by mountains.

Why has air quality improved so dramatically? Part of the answer lies in emissions targets set by federal, state, and local governments. But these need to be understood in the twin contexts of rising wealth and economic efficiency. As a Department of Interior analyst concluded after surveying emissions in 1999, "Cleaner air is a direct consequence of better technologies and the enormous and sustained investments that only a rich nation could have sunk into developing, installing, and operating these technologies." Today, American businesses, consumers, and government agencies spend about $40 billion annually on air pollution controls.

Wealth Makes for a Healthier Environment

It is now evident that countries undergo various environmental transitions as they become wealthier. *Fortune*'s special "ecology" edition in February 1970 was far more prescient than the doomsters when it noted, "If pollution is the brother of affluence, concern about pollution is affluence's child." In 1992, a World Bank analysis found that concentrations of particulates and sulfur dioxide peak at per capita incomes of $3,280 and $3,670, respectively. Once these income thresholds are crossed, societies start to purchase increased environmental amenities such as clean air and water.

In the U.S., air quality has been improving rapidly since before the first Earth Day—and before the federal Clean Air Act of 1970. In fact, ambient levels of particulates and sulfur dioxide have been declining ever since accurate records have been kept. Between 1960 and 1970, for instance, particulates declined by 25 percent; sulfur dioxide decreased by 35 percent between 1962 and 1970. More concretely, it takes 20 new cars to produce the same emissions that one car produced in the 1960s.

Similar trends can be found when it comes to water pollution. . . . Lake Erie once again supports a $600 million fishing industry. . . . The EPA estimates that between 60 percent and 70 percent of lakes, rivers, and streams meet state quality goals. That's up from about 30 percent to 40 percent 30 years ago.

In the U.S., air quality has been improving rapidly since before the first Earth Day—and before the federal Clean Air Act of 1970.

Since 1972, the United States has invested more than $540 billion in water pollution control efforts, according to the Pacific Research Center. In 1972, only 85 million Americans were served by sewage treatment plants. Since then, some 14,000 municipal waste treatment plants have been built and 173 million Americans are served by them. Similar air and water quality trends can be found in other developed countries as well. . . .

Extinction Theories Are Extinct

Worries about declining biodiversity have become popular lately. On the first Earth Day, participants were concerned about saving a few particularly charismatic species such as the bald eagle and the peregrine falcon. But even then some foresaw a coming holocaust. As Sen. Gaylord Nelson wrote in *Look*, "Dr. S. Dillon Ripley, secretary of the Smithsonian Institute, believes that in 25 years, somewhere between 75 and 80 percent of all the species of living animals will be extinct." Writing just five years after the first Earth Day, Paul Ehrlich and his biologist wife, Anne Ehrlich, predicted that "since more than nine-tenths of the original tropical rain-forests will be removed in most areas within the next 30 years or so, it is expected that half of the organisms in these areas will vanish with it."

There's only one problem: Most species that were alive in 1970 are still around today. "Documented animal extinctions peaked in the 1930s, and the number of extinctions has been declining since then," according to Stephen Edwards, an ecologist with the World Conservation Union, a leading international conservation organization whose members are nongovernmental organizations, international agencies, and national conservation agencies. Edwards notes that a 1994 World Conservation Union report found known extinctions since 1600 encompassed 258 animal species, 368 insect species, and 384 vascular plants. Most of these species, he explains, were "island endemics" like the Dodo. As a result, they are particularly vulnerable to habitat disruption, hunting, and competition from invading species. Since 1973, only seven species have gone extinct in the United States.

What mostly accounts for relatively low rates of extinction? As with many other green indicators, wealth leads the way by both creating a market for environmental values and delivering resource-efficient technology. Consider, for example, that one of the main causes of extinction is deforestation and the ensuing loss of habitat. According to the Consultative Group on International Agricultural Research, what drives most tropical deforestation is not commercial logging, but "poor farmers who have no other option for feeding their families than slashing and burning a patch of forest." By contrast, countries that practice high yield, chemically assisted agriculture have expanding forests. In 1920, U.S. forests covered 732 million acres. Today they cover 737 million acres, even though the number of Americans grew from 106 million in 1920 to 272 million now. Forests in Europe expanded even more dramatically, from 361 million acres to 482 million acres between 1950 and 1990. Despite continuing deforestation in tropical countries, Roger Sedjo, a senior fellow at the think tank Resources for the Future, notes that "76 percent of the tropical rain forest zone is still covered with forest." Which is quite a far cry from being nine-tenths gone. More good news: In its *State of the World's Forests 1999*, the U.N.'s Food and Agriculture Organization documents that while forests in developing countries were reduced by 9.1 percent between 1980 and 1995, the global rate of deforestation is now slowing.

"The developed countries in the temperate regions appear to have largely completed forestland conversion to agriculture and have achieved relative land use stability. By contrast, the developing countries in the tropics are still in a land conversion mode. This suggests that land conversion stability correlates strongly with successful economic development," concludes Sedjo, in his chapter on forestry in *The True State of the Planet*, a collection of essays I edited. In other words, if you want to save forests and wildlife, you had better help poor people become wealthy. . . .

Why so Wrong?

How did the doomsters get so many predictions so wrong on the first Earth Day? Their mistake can be handily summed up in Paul Ehrlich and John Holdern's infamous I = PAT equation. Impact (always negative) equals Population × Affluence × Technology, they declared. More people were *always* worse, by definition. Affluence meant that rich people were consuming more of the earth's resources, a concept that was regularly illustrated by claiming that the birth of each additional baby in America was worse for the environment than 25, 50, or even 60 babies born on the Indian subcontinent. And technology was bad because it meant that humans were pouring more poisons into the biosphere, drawing down more nonrenewable resources and destroying more of the remaining wilderness.

How did the doomsters get so many predictions so wrong on the first Earth Day?

We now know that Ehrlich and his fellow travelers got it backwards. If population were necessarily bad, then Brazil, with less than three-quarters the population density of the U.S., should be the wealthier society. As far as affluence goes, it is clearly the case that the richer the country, the cleaner the water, the clearer the air, and the more protected the forests. Additionally, richer countries also boast less hunger, longer lifespans, lower fertility rates, and more land set aside for nature. Relatively poor people can't afford to care overmuch for the state of the natural world.

With regards to technology, Ehrlich and other activists often claim that economists simply don't understand the simple facts of ecology. But it's the doomsters who need to update their economics—things have changed since the appearance of Thomas Malthus' 200-year-old *An Essay on the Principle of Population*, the basic text that continues to underwrite much apocalyptic rhetoric. Malthus hypothesized that while population increases geometrically, food and other resources increased arithmetically, leading to a world in which food was always in short supply. Nowadays, we understand that wealth is not created simply by combining land and labor. Rather, technological innovations greatly raise positive outputs in all sorts of ways while minimizing pollution and other negative outputs.

Indeed, if Ehrlich wants to improve his sorry record of predictions and his understanding of how to protect the natural world, he should walk across campus to talk with his Stanford University colleague, economist Paul Romer. "New Growth Theory," devised by Romer and others, shows that wealth springs from new ideas and new recipes. Romer sums it up this way: "Every generation has perceived the limits to growth that finite resources and undesirable side effects would pose if no new recipes or ideas were discovered. And every generation has underestimated the potential for finding new recipes and ideas. We consistently fail to grasp how many ideas remain to be discovered. The difficulty is the same one we have with compounding. Possibilities do not add up. They multiply." In other words, new ideas and technological recipes grow exponentially at a rate much faster than population does. . . .

If population were necessarily bad, then Brazil, with less than three-quarters the population density of the U.S., should be the wealthier society.

What will Earth look like when Earth Day 60 rolls around in 2030? Here are my predictions: As the International Food Policy Research Institute projects, we will be able to feed the world's additional numbers and to provide them with a better diet. Because they are ultimately political in nature, poverty and malnutrition will not be eliminated, but economic growth will make many people in the developing world much better off. Technological improvements in agriculture will mean less soil erosion, better management of freshwater supplies, and higher productivity crops. Life expectancy in the developing world will likely increase from 65 years to 73 years, and probably more; in the First World, it will rise to more than 80 years. Metals and mineral prices will be even lower than they are today. The rate of deforestation in the developing world will continue to slow down and forest growth in the developed economies will increase.

Meanwhile, as many developing countries become wealthier, they will start to pass through the environmental-transition thresholds for various pollutants, and their air and water quality will begin to improve. Certainly air and water quality in the United States, Europe, Japan, and other developed countries will be even better than it is today. Enormous progress will be made on the medical front, and diseases like AIDS and malaria may well be finally conquered. As for climate change, concern may be abating because the world's energy production mix is shifting toward natural gas and nuclear power. There is always the possibility that a technological breakthrough—say, cheap, efficient, non-polluting fuel cells—could radically reshape the energy sector. In any case a richer world will be much better able to cope with any environmental problems that might crop up.

One final prediction, of which I'm most absolutely certain: There will be a disproportionately influential group of doomsters predicting that the future—and the present—never looked so bleak.

The Extinction of Plants and Animals Is Not a Problem

Henry Lamb

About the author: Henry Lamb is executive vice president of the Environmental Conservation Organization, which promotes the protection of private property rights from erosion by excessive environmental regulations.

Someone has to say it out loud: the Endangered Species Act [ESA] is a disaster. In fact, it may be the stupidest law enacted since Prohibition [when the government outlawed the sale of alcoholic beverages]. Like Prohibition, the ESA reflects the will of a powerful minority, who prevail for a time, until the rest of the world realizes that the objective is unrealistic, and that the medicine is more deadly than the disease.

The bottom-feeding sucker fish in Klamath Lake has brought this issue into focus more clearly than the thousands of less prominent examples in recent years. The ESA declares that the sucker fish has more right to water than 1,400 farm families who depend upon that water for sustenance.

How stupid is that?

Step back a moment—from the sucker fish, the bald eagle, the grizzly bear, and the snail darter (and from the thousands of species no one has ever heard of)—and consider the idea this powerful minority of environmental extremists has been able to force upon the world with the ESA: Non-human species must be preserved no matter what the cost to humans.

This idea is even more stupid than the idea that government should prohibit humans from drinking "intoxicating liquors." The ESA seeks to prohibit nature from ending the existence of species.

Henry Lamb, "Repeal the ESA," www.worldnetdaily.com, July 11, 2001. Copyright © by WorldNetDaily.com, Inc. Reproduced by permission.

Unnatural Processes

Government could not stop people from drinking "intoxicating liquors"; it has no chance of preventing species from becoming extinct. Attempts to do so give rise to massive investment in unnatural processes that are destined to ultimate failure.

Suppose for a moment that the ESA were, or could be, successful. Would a better world result? I don't think so. To preserve all the species that happen to be on earth at this particular time in history would require an end to change. Progress would have to come to a screeching halt.

Would the world be a better place today, had the environmental extremists been in power, say 300 years ago, or a thousand years ago?

If the [Endangered Species Act] could be 100 percent successful today, it would be a tragedy for all who come after us.

Suppose for a moment that in order to preserve the non-human species, as the ESA seeks to do, progress had been halted by global decree in 1001. We would be looking at a life expectancy of, perhaps, 40 years. If we were very lucky, we might have a horse to transport us to a tavern where we might drink rot-gut whiskey to relieve the daily misery. Of course we would still have the pollution of the transportation system to deal with, as well.

Suppose progress had been stopped before Columbus arrived on this continent, which is the destination to which modern environmentalists say we should return. We might expect to live 45 years. Our food would be a daily struggle, and our transportation system would still be polluting by the shovel-full. Ah yes, a wonderful life for non-human species, perhaps, but a situation for humans to which only environmental wackos aspire.

Stopping Progress

If the ESA could be 100 percent successful today, it would be a tragedy for all who come after us. If we stop progress today, we condemn the people of future generations to the limits of our knowledge—and we have only begun to understand how wonderful life can be.

Nature intends for life on the planet to change. And it will—with or without the ESA. Do you think the ESA would have prevented extinction of the dinosaurs? Hardly. Change is progress. Human intervention in that process cannot improve the result, it can only slow the process.

The very idea of trying to save species flies in the face of the natural process. Environmental extremists contend that species loss is "unnatural" as the result of the habitat destruction by humans. This suggests that habitat modification by humans is not natural. How ridiculous. It is perfectly natural for humans to modify their habitat in any way their intellect and energy will allow. Inappropriate modifications bring natural consequences. Both human and non-human species learn from those consequences. Those species that can adapt through the learning process survive; those that fail to adapt, don't. Nor should they.

> The very idea of trying to save species flies in the face of the natural process.

If the condor can no longer live in its environment, nor find another suitable environment—so be it. Such a thought sends shivers down the spine of PETA [People for the Ethical Treatment of Animals] people, and others who hold non-human life to be of greater value than human life. They would contend that the "web of life" depends upon all species, and the loss of any species weakens the web that supports human life.

Extinction Is Natural

This argument has emotional sway, but fails the test of historic reality. This argument means that our life today would be better if dinosaurs still roamed the earth. How silly. The "web of life" lost a major chunk of its being when the dinosaurs departed the planet. I say good riddance; I'd hate to have to compete with those guys for food and shelter.

The planet will survive if the condor doesn't. The planet may no longer need whales, grizzly bears, or red-legged frogs. Believe it or not, the planet would survive even if the Klamath Lake sucker fish bit the dust. But the farmers, whose lives depend upon the water that accumulates in Klamath Lake, may not survive, if government continues its foolish effort to stop progress and preserve every species that some environmental extremist says is endangered.

Philosophically, the ESA is a flop. But the ESA is not really about saving species, this is only the sales pitch used to stir the emotions of humans who are suckers for a cuddly puppy dog, a kitty cat, a panda bear, or an injured anything. Environmental extremists have exploited the natural human compassion for animals, in order to use the law to torture humans whose behavior or lifestyle is different from what the environmentalists think it should be.

Managing Behavior

Similar to the teetotalers who used the law to torture humans whose behavior included taking a drink back in the roaring 20s, environmental extremists use the law to force other humans to behave as the environmentalists think they should.

Logging is a sin to environmental extremists; use the ESA to end logging. Mining is a sin to environmental extremists; use the ESA to end mining. Farming in the Klamath Basin is a sin to environmental extremists; use the ESA to end the farming. An ESA industry has arisen, which specializes in twisting the law to impose behavior modification on people who hold a different view.

It is time to send the ESA, and the industry it has spawned, into extinction.

It took 13 years to repeal the 18th Amendment (Prohibition). We have suffered under the ESA for nearly 30 years, but only in the last decade has it become the weapon of choice for environmental extremists. If the American people, in their collective wisdom, can overturn the extreme values of a powerful minority of teetotalers, the American people can overturn the values of a powerful minority of environmental extremists.

Our children and grandchildren will applaud us if we do, and curse us if we do not. The world will be a better place when we stop letting the extremists impose their views on the rest of us. It's time to tell your elected representatives to repeal the ESA, the modern prohibition to progress.

The Human Population Does Not Harm the Environment

Matt C. Abbott

About the author: Matt C. Abbott is a Catholic journalist and commentator.

During the last three decades, the issue of overpopulation—or perceived overpopulation—has been discussed in various capacities. The primary instigators of these discussions have been the radical environmentalists, the radical animal rights activists, and certain wealthy elites in our Western society. All of these groups more or less assert that human beings are destroying the planet. There are too many of us, they say. Hence, we must utilize "family planning" (read: abortion, contraception, sterilization), even in a coercive manner, to limit the number of people born into the world.

As a result of this elitist, anti-life mentality, also known as the "contraceptive mentality," several countries, including the U.S., are steeped in what the late Pope John Paul II called a culture of death. In third world countries, abortion, contraception and sterilization seemingly abound; yet the most basic needs of food, clean water and medicine are often lacking. Why is this so? It would seem that international organizations such as the United Nations and Planned Parenthood are more interested in reducing the population of those less fortunate than in working to promote authentic economic development in underdeveloped countries.

The primary instigators of these discussions [about human overpopulation] have been the radical environmentalists, the radical animal rights activists, and certain wealthy elites in our Western society. The main questions involving this matter, I submit, are these: Is the world indeed overpopulated? What

Matt C. Abbott, "The Population Control Controversy," www.renewamerica.com, June 2, 2005. Copyright © by Matt C. Abbott. Reproduced by permission.

can be done to promote economic development and responsible parenthood in a way that is morally acceptable to virtually everyone?

The Myth of Overpopulation

The assertion that the world is overpopulated is essentially a myth. In a January 29, 2005, address given by Cesare Bonivento, Roman Catholic bishop of Papua New Guinea, at the Family Life International Symposium held in Papua New Guinea, Bishop Bonivento cited a 2003 report issued by the United Nations Population Division warning that "future fertility levels in most developing countries will likely fall below 2.1 children per woman, the level needed to ensure the long-term replacement of the population. By 2050, the UN document says, three out of every four countries in the less developed regions will be experiencing below-replacement fertility, with all developed countries far below replacement level as well."

The primary instigators of these discussions [about human overpopulation] have been the radical environmentalists, the radical animal rights activists, and certain wealthy elites in our Western society.

Bishop Bonivento continued: "The deeper reductions in fertility will have as a consequence a faster aging of the population of developing countries, and this aging will stress social security systems. Globally, the number of older persons (60 years or over) will nearly triple, increasing from 606 million in 2000 to nearly 1.9 billion by 2050."

The UN's True Agenda

Interestingly, the United Nations Population Fund (UNFPA) released a report in 2004 predicting "that the world's population will increase by almost 40% by 2050, to 8.9 billion inhabitants" and that "such a demographic increase is an obstacle for development and for the environment."

Bishop Bonivento gave the following observation for the aforementioned contradictory report: "Why such an evidently contradictory evaluation? Because the warnings of the other UN agencies and of the demographers are jeopardizing UNFPA's effort to curb the population with any means, including legal abortion. UNFPA is the agency supporting the Chinese one-child policy, which includes forced abortion for women having a second child."

The assertion that the world is overpopulated is essentially a myth.

The assertion that the world is overpopulated is essentially a myth. Now, what can be done to foster economic development in third world countries? According to Dr. Brian Clowes, author and researcher for Human Life International, such a program would: "provide basic health care and prenatal care to women and children, thereby dramatically reducing infant mortality rates; build road systems and bridges to remote areas, thus promoting regional economic self-sufficiency; help break down artificial economic barriers, such as family-run utility monopolies and overly complicated procedures for securing permits in order to start small businesses, thereby stimulating healthy competition; improve agricultural production with rural electrification, mechanization and adequate grain storage, thereby improving nutrition; provide clean running water to villages, reducing endemic diseases; and provide basic education to those who are not receiving it."

Finally, the widespread promotion of natural family planning, also known as natural fertility regulation, is vital, as it is "morally acceptable to all religions and cultures". Information on natural family planning can be found on the following websites: www.ccli.org, www.popepaulvi.com.

CHAPTER 2

Should Global Warming Be Addressed?

Chapter Preface

Global warming has been the subject of much debate since the 1990s. Modern records dating back to the mid-nineteenth century indicate an increase in average global temperature of about 1.5 degrees over the past 150 years. Whether this increase is the result of human activities or whether such changes are part of natural climate variations is at the center of the debate. In deciding the validity of the arguments on both sides it is essential to evaluate the evidence; advocates on both sides of the debate, however, appear to be selective in the evidence they use to support their arguments.

Scientists attempt to determine historical temperatures in a variety of ways. One is to study the rings of ancient trees. Wider tree rings indicate a period of greater growth, which is usually a result of warmer temperatures. Ice core samples from glaciers and ice sheets also provide data about atmospheric gases and other climate indicators. Different types and amounts of oxygen in the water of the ice can suggest temperatures at the time the water froze. Archaeological evidence is also examined as scientists try to reconstruct ancient climates. For example, records kept by European vintners between A.D. 1100 and 1300 indicate that the climate then was sufficiently warm to allow for a thriving grape-growing industry in such currently unsuitably cold locations such as northern England, northern Germany, and northern France.

Proponents of the view that global warming is both a deviation from the norm and caused by human activity point to a graph created by scientist Michael Mann in the 1990s. The graph, a visual representation of average temperatures in the Northern Hemisphere from A.D. 1000 to the present, shows relatively stable temperatures until the twentieth century, at which point temperatures began a rapid increase. While Mann's modern data consisted of actual temperature readings, his historical data was taken largely from European tree rings. Mann's graph is commonly referred to as "the hockey stick" due to the sharp angle of the modern increase that follows the nearly straight historical line. Many scientists tie the modern increase to the emission of greenhouse gases produced by the burning of fossil fuels since the Industrial Revolution and especially since the advent of the internal combustion engine. According to author Bill McKibben, "If you drive an SUV, you're driving global warming."

Those who reject the theory of anthropogenic, or human-caused, global warming contend that indicators aside from European tree ring data indicate that a Little Ice Age and a Medieval Warm Period occurred, which undermines Mann's claims of a millennium of mostly stable temperatures. Instead of European tree-ring data, they used Tasmanian, Argentinean, and American tree ring data, oxygen isotopes in coral skeletons in the Caribbean, radio carbon dating of marine organisms in sea sediment in West Africa, and lake bed sediment in Kenya and China. Edward Cook of the Lamont-Doherty Earth Observatory notes, "Greenhouse gases added to the atmosphere by humans were not a factor back in the Medieval Warm Period."

The degree to which variations in global climate can be attributed to human-made causes will undoubtedly be studied and argued about for years to come. The authors of the viewpoints in this chapter debate whether global warming is a problem, what its causes are, and what its impact will be.

Global Warming Is a Serious Problem

Mark Lynas

About the author: *Mark Lynas, a broadcast commentator and journalist, is the author of* High Tide: News from a Warming World.

The first warning signs would have come from the sunsets. Weird splashes of red, yellow and purple-painted evening horizons all around the globe. Only those living near the eruption site would have seen the cause—vast volcanic outgassings of carbon dioxide, ash and sulphur. The end-Permian apocalypse had begun. By its conclusion, up to 95 per cent of species had been wiped out, the oceans transformed into black, oxygen-starved graveyards as millions of animal carcasses and uprooted plants rotted in the inky depths. It was the worst mass extinction ever to hit the planet, and it happened 251 million years ago because of global warming. (For a full description, see Michael Benton's *When Life Nearly Died*, published by Thames & Hudson last year [2003].)

Today, the world stands on the brink of a similar cataclysm, with one crucial difference. The agent of death at the end of the Permian period was volcanism. Now the agent of death is man.

A Looming Catastrophe

But how close are we to this catastrophe? Is it still avoidable? In the pre-industrial era, levels of carbon dioxide per cubic metre of air stood at roughly 278 parts per million (ppm). Today, they have soared to 376ppm, the highest in at least 420,000 years, and probably much longer. This means that ev-

Mark Lynas, "Global Warming: Is It Already Too Late?"*New Statesman*, May 17, 2004. Copyright © 2004 by the New Statesman, Ltd. Reproduced by permission.

ery breath of air we take is chemically different from the air breathed throughout the evolutionary history of the human species. And if the current rate of carbon accumulation continues, the rise in temperature could be as much as 6 [degrees] Celsius by the end of the century, according to the UN [United Nations] Intergovernmental Panel on Climate Change. That is roughly the same as the temperature increase that delivered the *coup de grace* to the prehistoric world of the Permian [period].

If the current rate of carbon accumulation continues, the rise in temperature could be as much as 6 [degrees] Celsius by the end of the century.

All the efforts of the climate-change panel, all the international conferences and protocols, all the green campaigning, are based on the assumption that, if we act now, the worst can be avoided. Although some global warming is already inescapable—temperatures will continue to rise for many years, and there is no power on earth that can stop them—we assume, none the less, that it is not too late; if we do the right things within the next couple of decades, temperatures will eventually stabilise.

An Unstoppable Force

But what if this is wrong? What if global warming is already unstoppable and is now accelerating uncontrollably? What if we have reached the point of no return and there is nothing we can do except wait for the end? Scientists are naturally cautious people, but a growing number fear that this may be the case. One ominous indicator comes from a US atmospheric sampling station 3,000 metres up on the northern flank of the Mauna Loa volcano in Hawaii. Since the 1950s, this station—and dozens of others dotted around the globe from Alaska to the South Pole—have recorded a steady increase in carbon-dioxide concentrations. The average year-on-year rise is 1.5ppm. Over the past two years [2002–2004], the rate of accumulation has doubled—to nearly 3ppm. This could mean that the rate of fossil-fuel burning has doubled—but it hasn't. The alternative explanation is that the biosphere "sinks", which used to absorb carbon, have suddenly shut down.

To understand the implications of this second possibility, we need to look at how global warming works. Every year, humans burn enough coal, oil and gas to add roughly six billion tonnes of carbon to the global atmosphere. This carbon was formerly trapped underground, laid down between rock deposits from much earlier (and warmer) phases in the earth's history. About half of this extra annual dose of carbon—three billion tonnes—is soaked up by oceans and plants. It is the other half that steadily accumulates in the atmosphere and causes all the trouble.

Every year, humans burn enough coal, oil and gas to add roughly six billion tonnes of carbon to the global atmosphere.

The fear is that, as temperatures rise, global warming, in a process that scientists call "positive feedback", will itself increase the amount of carbon released into the atmosphere, regardless of what humans do: in other words, the oceans and plants will stop soaking up those three billion tonnes. The UK [United Kingdom] Meteorological Office's Hadley Centre, which specialises in climate-change research, published an alarming paper in *Nature* in 2000 which gave the results of a computer simulation of the future global carbon cycle. It showed that if greenhouse-gas emissions continued, the Amazon rainforest ecosystem would begin to collapse, releasing vast quantities of stored carbon into the atmosphere in addition to the manmade carbon emissions. After about 2050, even more carbon would pour into the air from warming soils around the world. The combined effect would be enough to increase CO_2 in the atmosphere by another 250ppm—equivalent to a temperature rise of an extra 1.5 [degrees] Celsius above previous predictions.

Methane Burps

There is an even more chilling possibility. Deep under oceanic continental shelves right around the world, from Peru to Norway, huge quantities of methane are stored in "hydrate" form, kept solid by a combination of low temperatures and pressure from the water and sediment piled above them. It has been estimated that this methane hydrate store contains 10,000 gigatonnes—that is, ten thousand billion tonnes—of carbon, more than double the world's entire combined fossil-fuel reserves. Like carbon dioxide, methane is a greenhouse gas—in fact, it is 21 times more potent than CO_2. If even a small quantity were to escape into the atmosphere, runaway global warming might become inevitable.

This nightmare, scientists say, is increasingly likely. Warming ocean temperatures will destabilise the hydrates, allowing them to bubble up to the surface. This new methane will increase temperatures further, leading to still more release from the sea floor in a potentially unstoppable spiral. In fact, geologists increasingly think this feedback to have been the mechanism that drove the end-Permian cataclysm: carbon dioxide from volcanoes first raised world temperatures enough to destabilise methane hydrates, after which prehistoric global warming gained its own deadly momentum.

A more recent geological event, 55 million years ago at the end of the Palaeocene epoch, provides even stronger evidence that a "methane burp" from the oceans has indeed happened before. Although less dramatic than the end-Permian, it was also accompanied by mass extinctions. Indeed, it was in the recovery period from this second crisis that mammals—including our primate forebears—first exploded on to the scene.

The [British] government's chief scientist, Professor Sir David King, was referring to this period when he told reporters at [British prime minister] Tony Blair's Climate Group launch on 27 April [2004] that "Antarctica was the best place for mammals to live, and the rest of the globe would not sustain human life". He warned that these conditions, with CO_2 levels as high as 1,000ppm and no ice left on earth, could again be reached by 2100.

How seriously should we take these warnings? It must be emphasised that, while scientists are now virtually unanimous about the reality of man-made global warming—new evidence published in *Nature* that the troposphere, the lowest level of the atmosphere, is warming at roughly the same rate as the earth's surface has removed the last doubts—they are far more cautious about suggestions that it is already moving out of control. The increase in carbon-dioxide concentrations detected by the Hawaii station, says Pieter Tans of the US National Oceanic and Atmospheric Administration, may not continue. In warmer years, he explains, the rate of bacterial decomposition in the ground speeds up, and more carbon is released from soils. Over more than a few years, he says, ecosystems adjust. However, his colleague Ralph Keeling, while agreeing that the recent change "might not be such a big deal", points out that "there is no past period where the average carbon accumulation has stayed this high". Another expert on the carbon cycle—who was prepared to speak only on condition of anonymity—said: "We simply don't have a way to tell from just one year if a positive feedback is kicking in. But if it was happening, this is what it would look like."

That is the trouble with global warming. Human beings respond to events on a daily and weekly basis, not an annual, still less a decadal one. If enough [methane] gas is released, entire continental slopes could collapse in enormous submarine landslides, triggering tsunami waves of up to 15 metres in height. That is the trouble with global warming. Human beings respond to events on a daily and weekly basis, not an annual, still less a decadal one. But according to a paper from the Benfield Hazard Research Centre, . . . the impact of methane hydrate failure could be very dramatic indeed. If enough gas is released, entire continental slopes could collapse in enormous submarine landslides, triggering tsunami waves of up to 15 metres in height—enough to level entire coastal cities. Again, there is a precedent: just 7,000 years ago, an area of continental slope the size of Wales slid downhill between Norway and Iceland, triggering a tsunami that wiped out neolithic communities on the north-east coast of Scotland.

That is the trouble with global warming. Human beings respond to events on a daily and weekly basis, not an annual, still less a decadal one.

If such an event happens again, the only certainty is that there will be no warning. And yet, the danger signs are already all around: 2003 was the second-warmest year on record. Last summer's [2003's] heatwave across Europe was so far off the normal statistical scale that climatologists logged it as a once-in-10,000-years event. Sea-level rise is accelerating, according to the latest satellite measurements. And last month [April 2004], a truly unprecedented weather event occurred. Hurricanes were thought to be an entirely north Atlantic phenomenon. But on this occasion an Atlantic hurricane formed south of the Equator and struck Brazil with 90mph winds. Tropical meteorologists were so baffled that they had no idea what to call it, and hurricane monitoring systems may now have to be extended a thousand miles further south.

An Urgent Problem

So is there any hope of persuading politicians to treat global warming with the urgency it requires? Perhaps so, now that the story has reached Hollywood, with the disaster movie *The*

Day After Tomorrow.... Unfortunately, the events in the film are premised on an effect of global warming that remains contentious among scientists, and tends to confuse the public. This is the possibility that global warming, by increasing rainfall and ice-melt at high latitudes, shuts down the Atlantic's circulation, plunging Europe into a new ice age. A current known as the Gulf Stream transports a staggering amount of heat northwards, equivalent to the energy produced by about a million nuclear power stations. Without it, our climate would be between 5 [degrees] Celsius and 10 [degrees] Celsius colder—similar to that of Newfoundland. Again, the warning signs are clear: the "subpolar gyre" part of the current has already begun to slow, and through-flow of water between Iceland and the Faroes has declined by 20 per cent over the past 50 years.

However, *The Day After Tomorrow*'s storyline—where New York is flooded and then frozen solid within a week—is not even remotely likely. Most scientists, whilst quietly approving of Hollywood's sudden conversion to an issue that many have been battling to get into the media for years, give the film itself short shrift. Writing [in April 2004] in *Science* magazine, the oceanographer Andrew Weaver pooh-poohed the "new ice age" scenario, pointing out that such a drastic cooling of the climate would be impossible with greenhouse gases at today's elevated levels.

But whatever its flaws, there is at least a chance that the film will put global warming on the US political agenda. Indeed, the former vice-president, Al Gore, who frequently delivers speeches warning of the dangers of climate change, is planning a mass rally in New York City to capitalise on the sudden media interest.

The more common mood among environmentalists, however, is one of pessimism. At the annual UN climate-change talks, scheduled for Buenos Aires in December [2004], negotiators, instead of discussing "mitigation" (reducing greenhouse-gas emissions), are likely to focus mainly on "adaptation". In other words, having lost the battle to stop global warming, the best we can all now hope for is desperate rearguard actions to protect coastal land from flooding and to ward off large-scale starvation. Even the Pentagon is having to take note. A recent report for America's military top brass warned that mass refugee flows and competition for water and food could plunge the world into nuclear conflict. "Humans fight when they outstrip the carrying capacity of their natural environment," it warns. "The most combative societies are the ones that survive."

Abrupt Climate Change

The report charts some of the "potential military implications of climate change", including the collapse of the EU [European Union], civil war in China and the takeover of US borders by the army to prevent refugee incursions from the Caribbean and Mexico. The report's title, *Abrupt Climate Change*, reflects an increasing awareness among scientists and policymakers alike that global warming is more likely to lead to sudden climatic shifts than to slow, linear change. Once more, the earth's climate history gives a precedent: the planet swung between cold and warm periods at the end of the most recent ice age in as little as a decade.

Sudden, unanticipated events—which climatologists drily term "surprises"—could include, for example, the collapse of the west Antarctic ice sheet and the catastrophic inundation of low-lying areas all around the world. This is the scenario that causes giant waves to flood Manhattan in *The Day After Tomorrow*. In reality, even the most dramatic rise in sea level would still take years rather than minutes to flood coastal cities.

A better storyline might have run as follows. Rapid melting of the Greenland ice sheet causes the offshore continental shelf to rebound upwards, releasing huge quantities of methane hydrates with explosive force. The entire shelf slumps downward, triggering 15m-high tsunamis right across the north Atlantic, wiping out Reykjavik, Lisbon and—ultimately—New York City itself. The new methane adds rapidly to global warming, causing mega-droughts and mass starvation across Asia, Africa and South America. Don't forget: it's happened before, so it could happen again.

Three months ago, scientists would have laughed if a film had portrayed a freak hurricane forming in the south Atlantic. Now nobody's smiling.

Greenhouse Gas Emissions Can Be Reduced Without Harming the Economy

Arnold Schwarzenegger

About the author: Arnold Schwarzenegger is the governor of California.

I don't know how apparent it is to people in Britain, but California has long been a leader in environmental protection. We have never taken for granted the clean air, clean water and natural beauty that make our state such a desirable place to live, to work, and to raise our families. That's why, when I became Governor of California, I announced a bold agenda to continue and strengthen our commitment to meeting the many environmental challenges we face.

During the past 18 months, we created the 25 million-acre Sierra Nevada Conservancy, the largest conservancy in the nation; we opened the path to the Hydrogen Highway, which will encourage the building of hydrogen fuelling stations and the use of hydrogen-fuelled vehicles; we sponsored the first Ocean Protection Act in the nation to protect and restore our ocean resources; and we secured permanent funding to reduce emissions from dirty engines and equipment.

In addition, with our Green Building Initiative, we have put the biggest user of electricity in California "the state government itself" on an energy diet. By requiring new state buildings to use the latest environmentally friendly and energy efficient design and construction methods, we will reduce electricity and water use by more than 20 per cent in our state-owned facilities.

Arnold Schwarzenegger, "G8: It's Not Time For a Talk. It's Time For Action," *Independent on Sunday*, July 3, 2005. Copyright © 2005 by Independent Newspapers (UK) Ltd. Reproduced by permission.

The Debate Is Over

Now it is time for Californians to seriously address the issue of climate change and its potential to create havoc with our environment and economy. The debate is over. We know the science. We see the threat posed by changes in our climate. And we know the time for action is now.

I launched our effort when California hosted the United Nations World Environment Day Conference in San Francisco last month [June 2005], where leaders from around the world gathered to discuss our shared responsibility for protecting the earth. It was there that I signed an executive order to establish clear and ambitious goals to reduce greenhouse gas emissions in our state: by the year 2010 our goal is to reduce our emissions to less than those we produced in 2000; by 2020 our goal is to make our emissions lower than 1990 levels; and by 2050 our goal is to reduce overall emissions to a full 80 per cent below those we produced in 1990.

We have no choice but to take action to reduce greenhouse gas emissions. Greenhouse gases are emitted from every sector of the economy, and these pollutants blanket the globe, trapping heat and creating the "greenhouse" effect, often referred to as global warming. Global warming threatens California's water supply, public health, agriculture, coastlines and forests—our entire economy and way of life. We have no choice but to take action to reduce greenhouse gas emissions.

We have no choice but to take action to reduce green-house gas emissions.

In order to achieve our goals, we are implementing California's landmark greenhouse gas law, which requires lower-emitting vehicles to be sold in our state, starting in 2009. We are accelerating the timetable to get more energy from renewable resources, such as wind, solar, geo-thermal and bio-mass conversion to 20 per cent by 2010 and 33 per cent by 2020. We have implemented the world's most stringent appliance and building efficiency standards. We are aggressively pursuing with the legislature my proposal to have one million solar-powered homes and buildings in California to save energy and reduce pollution. We are greening the state's fleet of government vehicles, to be the most fuel-efficient in the world.

Pollution Reduction Is a Money-Maker

These steps are great for the environment and great for our economy, too. Many people have falsely assumed that you have to choose between protecting the environment and protecting the economy. Nothing could be further from the truth. In California, we will do both.

That is why I am travelling around the state and my administration is holding a series of conservation summits for businesses around California, spreading the word that pollution reduction is good.

Pollution reduction has long been a money saver for businesses. It lowers operating costs, raises profits and creates new and expanded markets for environmental technology.

Many private businesses in California are cutting greenhouse gas emissions by simply improving efficiency. Others are also implementing cutting-edge hydrogen fuel technologies, installing advanced solar power systems and constructing environmentally friendly buildings.

And best of all, many California companies are participating in the public and private partnerships that are being formed with the state and some of our leading universities and research centres to find innovative means to create a cleaner and healthier environment.

A Cleaner, Healthier Tomorrow

All of these environmental technologies will allow us to conserve energy, cut pollution, protect our natural resources and create jobs for Californians. We must all accept the challenge to protect our environment. In California, I am pleased that we are once again providing leadership in this critical area. We understand that in this world in which we live, our actions sometimes have unintended consequences for our land, air and water. As John Muir, an immigrant from your islands who launched America's conservation movement here in California, once said: "When one tugs at a single thing in nature he finds it attached to the rest of the world." I ask citizens and governments everywhere to do their part by conserving energy, reducing the use of fossil fuels, reducing waste and taking every opportunity to work together for a cleaner, healthier tomorrow. It is not enough for us to be just caretakers of the world that we have been given, we must leave it a better place for future generations.

This is our duty to those who share this world with us and to those who follow us.

Global Warming Is Caused by Human Activities

Thomas R. Karl and Kevin E. Trenberth

About the authors: Thomas R. Karl is director of the National Climatic Data Center in Asheville, North Carolina. Kevin E. Trenberth heads the climate analysis section of the National Center for Atmospheric Research in Boulder, Colorado.

The atmosphere is a global commons that responds to many types of emissions into it, as well as to changes in the surface beneath it. As human balloon flights around the world illustrate, the air over a specific location is typically halfway around the world a week later, making climate change a truly global issue.

Over the past 50 years, human influences have been the dominant detectable influence on climate change.

Planet Earth is habitable because of its location relative to the sun and because of the natural greenhouse effect of its atmosphere. Various atmospheric gases contribute to the greenhouse effect, whose impact in clear skies is ~60% from water vapor, ~25% from carbon dioxide, ~8% from ozone, and the rest from trace gases including methane and nitrous oxide. Clouds also have a greenhouse effect. On average, the energy from the sun received at the top of the Earth's atmosphere amounts to 175 petawatts (PW) (or 175 quadrillion watts), of which ~31% is reflected by clouds and from the surface. The rest (120 PW) is absorbed by the atmosphere, land, or ocean and ultimately emitted back to space as infrared radiation. Over the past century, infrequent volcanic eruptions of gases and debris into the atmosphere have significantly perturbed these energy flows; however, the resulting cooling has lasted for only a few years. Inferred changes in total solar irradiance

Thomas R. Karl and Kevin E. Trenberth, "Modern Global Climate Change," *Science*, vol. 302, December 5, 2003. Copyright © 2003 by the American Association for the Advancement of Science. Reproduced by permssion.

appear to have increased global mean temperatures by perhaps as much as 0.2[degrees] C in the first half of the 20th century, but measured changes in the past 25 years are small. Over the past 50 years, human influences have been the dominant detectable influence on climate change. The following briefly describes the human influences on climate, the resulting temperature and precipitation changes, the time scale of responses, some important processes involved, the use of climate models for assessing the past and making projections into the future, and the need for better observational and information systems.

Over the past 50 years, human influences have been the dominant detectable influence on climate change.

The main way in which humans alter global climate is by interference with the natural flows of energy through changes in atmospheric composition, not by the actual generation of heat in energy usage. On a global scale, even a 1% change in the energy flows, which is the order of the estimated change to date, dominates all other direct influences humans have on climate. For example, an energy output of just one PW is equivalent to that of a million power stations of 1000-MW capacity, among the largest in the world. Total human energy use is about a factor of 9000 less than the natural flow.

---

*Global changes in atmospheric composition occur
... from multiple human activities.*

Greenhouse Gases

Global changes in atmospheric composition occur from anthropogenic emissions of greenhouse gases, such as carbon dioxide that results from the burning of fossil fuels and methane and nitrous oxide from multiple human activities. Because these gases have long (decades to centuries) atmospheric life-times, the result is an accumulation in the atmosphere and a buildup in concentrations that are clearly shown both by in-strumental observations of air samples since 1958 and in bubbles of air trapped in ice cores before then. Moreover, these gases are well distributed in the atmosphere across the globe, simplifying a global monitoring strategy. Carbon diox-ide has increased 31% since preindustrial times, from 280 parts per million by volume (ppmv) to more than 370 ppmv today, and half of the increase has been since 1965. The green-house gases trap outgoing radiation from the Earth to space, creating a warming of the planet. . . .

Human activities also have a large-scale impact on the land surface. Changes in land-use through urbanization and agricultural practices, although not global, are often most pro-nounced where people live, work, and grow food, and are part of the human impact on climate. Large-scale deforestation and desertification in Amazonia and the Sahel, respectively, are two instances where evidence suggests there is likely to be human influence on regional climate. In general, city climates differ from those in surrounding rural green areas, because of the "concrete jungle" and its effects on heat retention, runoff, and pollution, resulting in urban heat islands.

Human Influences

There is no doubt that the composition of the atmosphere is changing because of human activities, and today greenhouse gases are the largest human influence on global climate. Re-cent greenhouse gas emissions trends in the United States are upward, as are global emissions trends, with increases between 0.5 and 1% per year over the past few decades. Concentra-tions of both reflective and nonreflective aerosols are also esti-mated to be increasing. Because radiative forcing from green-house gases dominates over the net cooling forcings from aerosols, the popular term for the human influence on global climate is "global warming," although it really means global heating, of which the observed global temperature increase is only one consequence. Already it is estimated that the Earth's climate has exceeded the bounds of natural variability, and this has been the case since about 1980.

Changes in land-use through urbanization and agricultural practices ... are part of the human impact on climate.

Surface moisture, if available (as it always is over the oceans), effectively acts as the "air conditioner" of the surface, as heat used for evaporation moistens the air rather than warming it. Therefore, another consequence of global heating of the lower troposphere is accelerated land-surface drying and more atmospheric water vapor (the dominant greenhouse gas). Accelerated drying increases the incidence and severity of droughts, whereas additional atmospheric water vapor increases the risk of heavy precipitation events. Basic theory, climate model simulations, and empirical evidence all confirm that warmer climates, owing to increased water vapor, lead to more intense precipitation events even when the total precipitation remains constant, and with prospects for even stronger events when precipitation amounts increase.

There is considerable uncertainty as to exactly how anthropogenic global heating will affect the climate system, how long it will last, and how large the effects will be. Climate has varied naturally in the past, but today's circumstances are unique because of human influences on atmospheric composition. As we progress into the future, the magnitude of the present anthropogenic change will become overwhelmingly large compared to that of natural changes. In the absence of climate mitigation policies, the 90% probability interval for warming from 1990 to 2100 is 1.7 [degrees] to 4.9 [degrees] C. About half of this range is due to uncertainty in future

Horses graze near Ratcliffe on Soar power station in central England. © Darren Staples/ Reuters/CORBIS

emissions and about half is due to uncertainties in climate models, especially in their sensitivity to forcings that are complicated by feedbacks, discussed below, and in their rate of heat uptake by the oceans. Even with these uncertainties, the likely outcome is more frequent heat waves, droughts, extreme precipitation events, and related impacts (such as wild fires, heat stress, vegetation changes, and sea level rise) that will be regionally dependent.

Rapid Climate Change

The rate of human-induced climate change is projected to be much faster than most natural processes, certainly those prevailing over the past 10,000 years. Thresholds likely exist that, if crossed, could abruptly and perhaps almost irreversibly switch the climate to a different regime. Such rapid change is evident in past climates during a slow change in the Earth's orbit and tilt, such as the Younger Dryas cold event from ~11,500 to ~12,700 years ago, perhaps caused by freshwater discharges from melting ice sheets into the North Atlantic Ocean and a change in the ocean thermohaline circulation. The great ice sheets of Greenland and Antarctica may not be stable, because the extent to which cold-season heavier snow-fall partially offsets increased melting as the climate warms remains uncertain. A combination of ocean temperature increases and ice sheet melting could systematically inundate the world's coasts by raising sea level for centuries.

Given what has happened to date and is projected in the future, substantial further climate change is guaranteed. The rate of change can be slowed, but it is unlikely to be stopped in the 21st century. Because concentrations of long-lived greenhouse gases are dominated by accumulated past emissions, it takes many decades for any change in emissions to have much effect. This means the atmosphere still has unrealized warming (estimated to be at least another 0.5 [degrees]C) and that sea level rise may continue for centuries after an abatement of anthropogenic greenhouse gas emissions and the stabilization of greenhouse gas concentrations in the atmosphere.

Natural Feedback

Our understanding of the climate system is complicated by feedbacks that either amplify or dampen perturbations, the most important of which involve water in various phases. As temperatures increase, the water-holding capacity of the atmosphere increases along with water vapor amounts, producing water vapor feedback. As water vapor is a strong greenhouse gas, this diminishes the loss of energy through increased radiation to space. Currently, water vapor feedback is estimated to contribute a radiative effect from one to two times the size of the direct effect of increases in anthropogenic greenhouse gases. Precipitation-runoff feedbacks occur because more intense rains run off at the expense of soil moisture, and warming promotes rain rather than snow. These changes in turn alter the partitioning of solar radiation into sensible versus latent heating. Heat storage feedbacks include the rate at which the oceans take up heat and the currents redistribute and release it back into the atmosphere at variable later times and different locations.

Given what has happened to date and is projected in the future, substantial further climate change is guaranteed.

Cloud feedback occurs because clouds both reflect solar radiation, causing cooling, and trap outgoing long-wave radiation, causing warming. Depending on the height, location, and the type of clouds with their related optical properties, changes in cloud amount can cause either warming or cooling. Future changes in clouds are the single biggest source of uncertainty in climate predictions. They contribute to an uncertainty in the sensitivity of models to changes in greenhouse gases, ranging from a small negative feedback, thereby slightly reducing the direct radiative effects of increases in greenhouse gases, to a doubling of the direct radiative effect of increases in greenhouse gases. Clouds and precipitation processes cannot be resolved in climate models and have to be parametrically represented (parameterized) in terms of variables that are resolved. This will continue for some time into the future, even with projected increases in computational capability.

Ice-albedo feedback occurs as increased warming diminishes snow and ice cover, making the planet darker and more receptive to absorbing incoming solar radiation, causing warming, which further melts snow and ice. This effect is greatest at high latitudes. Decreased snow cover extent has significantly contributed to the earlier onset of spring in the past few decades over northern-hemisphere high latitudes. Ice-albedo feedback is affected by changes in clouds, thus complicating the net feedback effect.

Predicting Climate Change

The primary tools for predicting future climate are global climate models, which are fully coupled, mathematical, computer-based models of the physics, chemistry, and biology of the atmosphere, land surface, oceans, and cryosphere and their interactions with each other and with the sun and other influences (such as volcanic eruptions). Outstanding issues in modeling include specifying forcings of the climate system; properly dealing with complex feedback processes that affect carbon, energy, and water sources, sinks and transports; and improving simulations of regional weather, especially extreme events. Today's inadequate or incomplete measurements of various forcings, with the exception of well-mixed greenhouse gases, add uncertainty when trying to simulate past and present climate. Confidence in our ability to predict future climate is dependent on our ability to use climate models to attribute past and present climate change to specific forcings. Through clever use of paleoclimate data, our ability to reconstruct past forcings should improve, but it is unlikely to provide the regional detail necessary that comes from long-term direct measurements. An example of forcing uncertainty comes from recent satellite observations and data analyses of 20th-century surface, upper air, and ocean temperatures, which indicate that estimates of the indirect effects of sulfate aerosols on clouds may be high, perhaps by as much as a factor of two. Human behavior, technological change, and the rate of population growth also affect future emissions and our ability to predict these must be factored into any long-term climate projection. . . .

Entering the Unknown

In large part, reduction in uncertainty about future climate change will be driven by studies of climate change assessment and attribution. Along with climate model simulations of past climates, this requires comprehensive and long-term climate-related data sets and observing systems that deliver data free of time-dependent biases. These observations would ensure that model simulations are evaluated on the basis of actual changes in the climate system and not on artifacts of changes in observing system technology or analysis methods. The recent controversy regarding the effects that changes in observing systems have had on the rate of surface versus tropospheric warming highlights this issue. Global monitoring through space-based and surface-based systems is an international matter, much like global climate change. There are encouraging signs, such as the adoption in 1999 of a set of climate monitoring principles, but these principles are impotent without implementation. International implementation of these principles is spotty at best.

We are entering the unknown with our climate. We need a global climate observing system, but only parts of it exist. We must not only take the vital signs of the planet but also assess why they are fluctuating and changing. Consequently, the system must embrace comprehensive analysis and assessment as integral components on an ongoing basis, as well as innovative research to better interpret results and improve our diagnostic capabilities. Projections into the future are part of such activity, and all aspects of an Earth information system feed into planning for the future, whether by planned adaptation or mitigation. Climate change is truly a global issue, one that may prove to be humanity's greatest challenge. It is very unlikely to be adequately addressed without greatly improved international cooperation and action.

Global Warming Is Not a Serious Problem

Thomas Sieger Derr

About the author: Thomas Sieger Derr is a professor of religion and ethics at Smith College and the author of Environmental Ethics and Christian Humanism.

Global warming has achieved the status of a major threat. It inspires nightmares of a troubled future and propels apocalyptic dramas such as the summer 2004 movie *The Day After Tomorrow*. Even were the Kyoto treaty [to reduce greenhouse gas emissions] to be fully implemented, it wouldn't make a dent in the warming trend, which seems to be inexorable. Doom is upon us.

Scientists familiar with the issues involved have written critically about the theory of global warming. Except that maybe it isn't. You might not know it from ordinary media accounts, which report the judgments of alarmists as "settled science," but there is a skeptical side to the argument. Scientists familiar with the issues involved have written critically about the theory of global warming. The puzzle is why these commentators, well-credentialed and experienced, have been swept aside to produce a false "consensus." What is it that produces widespread agreement among both "experts" and the general public on a hypothesis which is quite likely wrong?

The consensus holds that we are experiencing unprecedented global warming and that human activity is the main culprit. The past century, we are told, has been the hottest on record, with temperatures steadily rising during the last decades. Since human population and industrial activity have risen at the same time, it stands to reason that human activity

Thomas Sieger Derr, "Strange Science," *First Things: A Monthly Journal of Religion and Public Life,* November 2004, p. 5. Copyright © 2004 by the Institute on Religion and Public Life. Reproduced by permission.

is, one way or another, the cause of this observed warming. Anything wrong with this reasoning?

Faulty Assumptions

Quite a lot, as it turns out. The phrase "on record" doesn't mean very much, since most records date from the latter part of the nineteenth century. Without accurate records there are still ways of discovering the temperatures of past centuries, and these methods do not confirm the theory of a steady rise. Reading tree rings helps (the rings are further apart when the temperature is warmer and the trees grow faster). Core samples from drilling in ice fields can field even older data. Some historical reconstruction can help, too—for example, we know that the Norsemen settled Greenland (and named it "green") a millennium ago and grew crops there, in land which is today quite inhospitable to settlement, let alone to agriculture. Other evidence comes from coral growth, isotope data from sea floor sediment, and insects, all of which point to a very warm climate in medieval times. Abundant testimony tells us that the European climate then cooled dramatically from the thirteenth century until the eighteenth, when it began its slow rewarming.

In sum, what we learn from multiple sources is that the earth (and not just Europe) was warmer in the tenth century than it is now, that it cooled dramatically in the middle of our second millennium (this has been called the "little ice age"), and then began warming again. Temperatures were higher in medieval times (from about 800 to 1300) than they are now, and the twentieth century represented a recovery from the little ice age to something like normal. The false perception that the recent warming trend is out of the ordinary is heightened by its being measured from an extraordinarily cold starting point, without taking into account the earlier balmy medieval period, sometimes called the Medieval Climate Optimum. Data such as fossilized sea shells indicate that similar natural climate swings occurred in prehistoric times, well before the appearance of the human race.

The earth (and not just Europe) was warmer in the tenth century than it is now.

Even the period for which we have records can be misread. While the average global surface temperature increased by about 0.5 degrees Celsius during the twentieth century, the major part of that warming occurred in the early part of the century, before the rapid rise in human population and before the consequent rise in emissions of polluting substances into the atmosphere. There was actually a noticeable cooling period after World War II, and this climate trend produced a rather different sort of alarmism—some predicted the return of an ice age. In 1974 the National Science Board, observing a thirty-year-long decline in world temperature, predicted the end of temperate times and the dawning of the next glacial age. Meteorologists, *Newsweek* reported, were "almost unanimous in the view that the trend will reduce agricultural productivity for the rest of the century." But they were wrong, as we now know (another caution about supposedly "unanimous" scientific opinion), and after 1975 we began to experience our current warming trend. Notice that these fluctuations, over the centuries and within them, do not correlate with human numbers or activity. They are evidently caused by something else.

Sketchy Evidence

The evidence that greenhouse gasses produced by human beings are causing any significant warming is sketchy. What, then, is the cause of the current warming trend? As everyone has heard, the emission of so-called "greenhouse gasses," mostly carbon dioxide from burning fossil fuels, is supposed to be the major culprit in global warming. This is the anthropogenic hypothesis, according to which humans have caused the trouble. But such emissions correlate with human numbers and industrial development, so they could not have been the cause of warming centuries ago, nor of the nineteenth-century rewarming trend which began with a much smaller human population and before the industrial revolution. Nor is there a very good correlation between atmospheric carbon dioxide levels and past climate changes. Thus, to many scientists, the evidence that greenhouse gasses produced by humans are causing any significant warming is sketchy.

The evidence that greenhouse gasses produced by human beings are causing any significant warming is sketchy.

The likeliest cause of current climate trends seems to be solar activity, perhaps in combination with galactic cosmic rays caused by supernovas, especially because there is some good observable correlation between solar magnetism output and terrestrial climate change. But that kind of change is not predictable within any usable time frame, not yet anyway, and, of course, it is entirely beyond any human influence. The conclusion, then, is that the climate will change naturally; aside from altering obviously foolish behavior, such as releasing dangerous pollutants into our air and water, we can and should do little more than adapt to these natural changes, as all life has always done.

Benefits of Global Warming

That is not a counsel of despair, however, for global warming is not necessarily a bad thing; and higher levels of carbon dioxide help plants to grow (carbon dioxide is not a pollutant), and, indeed, mapping by satellite shows that the earth has become about six percent greener overall in the past two decades, with forests expanding into arid regions (though the effect is uneven). The Amazon rain forest was the biggest gainer, despite the much-advertised deforestation caused by human cutting along its edges. Certainly climate change does not help every region equally and will probably harm some. That has always been true. But there are careful studies that predict overall benefit to the earth with increasing warmth: fewer storms (not more), more rain, better crop yields over larger areas, and longer growing seasons, milder winters, and decreasing heating costs in colder latitudes. The predictable change, though measurable, will not be catastrophic at all—maybe one degree Celsius during the twenty-first century. The news is certainly not all bad, and may on balance be rather good.

Increasing warmth and higher levels of carbon dioxide help plants to grow.

There is much more, in more detail, to the argument of those scientists who are skeptical about the threat of global warming. On the whole, their case is, I think, quite persuasive. The question, then, is why so few people believe it.

The media report arresting and frightening items, for that is what draws listeners, viewers, and readers. Part of the answer is that bad news is good news—for the news media. The purveyors of climate disaster theories have exploited this journalistic habit quite brilliantly, releasing steadily more frightening scenarios without much significant data to back them up. Consider the unguarded admission of Steven Schneider of Stanford, a leading proponent of the global warming theory. In a now notorious comment, printed in *Discover* in 1989 and, surely to his discomfort, often cited by his opponents, Schneider admitted: To capture the public imagination, we have to offer up scary scenarios, make simplified dramatic statements, and make little mention of any doubts we may have. Each of us has to decide what the right balance is between being effective and being honest.

This sort of willingness to place the cause above the truth has exasperated Richard Lindzen, Sloan Professor of Meteorology at MIT [Massachusetts Institute of Technology], who is one of the authors of the science sections of the report of the International Panel on Climate Change (IPCC), the body responsible for an increasing crescendo of dire warnings. In testimony before the U.S. Senate's Environment and Public Works Committee, he called the IPCC's Summary for Policymakers, which loudly sounds the warming alarm, "very much a child's exercise of what might possibly happen . . . [which] conjures up some scary scenarios, for which, there is no evidence."

This brings us to the second part of the answer, which concerns the political and economic consequences of the policy argument. The IPCC is a UN [United Nations] body and reflects UN politics, which are consistently favorable to developing countries, the majority of its members. Those politics are very supportive of the Kyoto treaty, which not only exempts the developing countries from emissions standards but also requires compensatory treatment from the wealthier nations for any economic restraints that new climate management policies may impose on these developing countries. Were Kyoto to be implemented as written, the developing countries would gain lots of money and free technology. One need not be a cynic to grasp that a UN body will do obeisance to these political realities wherever possible.

The Kyoto Failure

The Kyoto treaty would not make a measurable difference in the climate—by 2050, a temperature reduction of maybe two-hundredths of a degree Celsius, or at most six-hundredths of a degree—but the sacrifices it would impose on the United States would be quite large. It would require us to reduce our projected 2012 energy use by 25 percent, a catastrophic economic hit. Small wonder that the Senate in 1997 passed a bipartisan resolution, the Byrd-Hagel anti-Kyoto resolution, by

95-0 (a fact rarely recalled by those who claim that America's refusal to sign on to the treaty was the result of the Bush administration's thralldom to corporate interests).

Most of the European countries that have ratified Kyoto are falling behind already on targets, despite having stagnant economies and falling populations. It is highly unlikely they will meet the goals they have signed on for, and they know it. Neither will Japan, for that matter. The European Union has committed itself to an eight percent reduction in energy use (from 1990 levels) by 2012, but the European Environment Agency admits that current trends project only a 4.7 percent reduction. When Kyoto signers lecture non-signers for not doing enough for the environment, they invite the charge of hypocrisy. There is also the obvious fact that adherence to the treaty will hurt the U.S. economy much more than the European, which suggests that old-fashioned economic competitiveness is in the mix of motives at play here. The absurdity of the treaty becomes obvious when we recognize that it does not impose emissions requirements on developing countries, including economic giants such as China, India, and Brazil. (China will become the world's biggest source of carbon dioxide emissions in just a few years.)

A third reason why global warming fears seem to be carrying the day goes beyond these political interests; it involves intellectual pride. Academics are a touchy tribe (I'm one of them); they do not take it kindly when their theories, often the result of hard work, are contradicted. And sure enough, the struggle for the truth in this matter is anything but polite. It is intellectual warfare, entangled with politics, reputations, and ideology; and most of the anger comes from the side of the alarmists. People lose their tempers and hurl insults— "junk science," "willful ignorance," "diatribe," "arrogant," "stupid," "incompetent," "bias," "bad faith," "deplorable misinformation," and more. Consider the fiercely hateful reaction to Bjorn Lomborg's 2001 book, *The Skeptical Environmentalist.*

He challenged the entrenched and politically powerful ortho-doxy and did so with maddeningly thorough data. His critics, unable to refute his statistics, seem to have been enraged by their own weakness—a familiar phenomenon, after all. Or perhaps, with their reputations and their fund-raising ability tied to the disaster scenarios, they felt their livelihoods threat-ened. In any case, the shrillness of their voices has helped to drown out the skeptics.

The Evils of Modern Civilization

The global warming campaign is the leading edge of an envi-ronmentalism which goes far beyond mere pollution control and indicts the global economy. Finally, there is a fourth cause: a somewhat murky antipathy to modern technological civili-zation as the destroyer of a purer, cleaner, more "natural" life, a life where virtue dwelt before the great degeneration set in. The global warming campaign is the leading edge of an envi-ronmentalism which goes far beyond mere pollution control and indicts the global economy for its machines, its agribusi-ness, its massive movements of goods, and above all its grow-ing population. Picking apart this argument to show the weak-ness of its pieces does not go to the heart of the fear and loathing that motivate it. The revulsion shows in the prescrip-tions advanced by the global warming alarmists: roll back emissions to earlier levels; reduce production and consump-tion of goods; lower birth rates. Our material ease and the freedoms it has spawned are dangerous illusions, bargains with the devil, and now comes the reckoning. A major apoca-lypse looms, either to destroy or, paradoxically, to save us—if we come to our senses in the nick of time.

It is clear, then, given the deep roots of the scare, that it is likely to be pretty durable. It has the added advantage of not being readily falsifiable in our lifetimes; only future humans, who will have the perspective of centuries, will know for cer-tain whether the current warming trend is abnormal. In the meantime, the sanest course for us would be to gain what limited perspective we can (remembering the global cooling alarm of a generation ago) and to proceed cautiously. We are going through a scare with many causes, and we need to step back from it, take a long second look at the scientific evidence, and not do anything rash. Though the alarmists claim otherwise, the science concerning global warming is certainly not settled. It is probable that the case for anthropogenic warming will not hold up, and that the earth is behaving as it has for millennia, with natural climate swings that have little to do with human activity.

Reducing Greenhouse Gases Would Harm the Economy

James Inhofe

About the author: James Inhofe is a U.S. senator representing Oklahoma.

Much of the debate over global warming is predicated on fear, rather than science. Global warming alarmists see a future plagued by catastrophic flooding, war, terrorism, economic dislocations, droughts, crop failures, mosquito-borne diseases, and harsh weather—all caused by man-made greenhouse gas emissions.

Hans Blix, chief UN [United Nations] weapons inspector, sounded both ridiculous and alarmist when he said in March [2003], "I'm more worried about global warming than I am of any major military conflict."

Much of the debate over global warming is predicated on fear, rather than science.

Science writer David Appell, who has written for such publications as the *New Scientist* and *Scientific American*, parroted Blix when he said global warming would "threaten fundamental food and water sources. It would lead to displacement of billions of people and huge waves of refugees, spawn terrorism and topple governments, spread disease across the globe."

Appell's next point deserves special emphasis, because it demonstrates the sheer lunacy of environmental extremists: "[Global warming] would be chaos by any measure, far greater even than the sum total of chaos of the global wars of the 20th century, and so in this sense Blix is right to be concerned. Sounds like a weapon of mass destruction to me."

James Inhofe, address before the U.S. Senate, Washington, D.C., July 28, 2003.

No wonder the late political scientist Aaron Wildavsky called global warming alarmism the "mother of all environmental scares."

Appell and Blix sound very much like those who warned us in the 1970s that the planet was headed for a catastrophic global *cooling*. On April 28, 1975, *Newsweek* printed an article titled, "The Cooling World," in which the magazine warned: "There are ominous signs that the earth's weather patterns have begun to change dramatically and that these changes may portend a drastic decline in food production, with serious political implications for just about every nation on earth."

In a similar refrain, *Time* magazine for June 24, 1974 declared: "However widely the weather varies from place to place and time to time, when meteorologists take an average of temperatures around the globe they find that the atmosphere has been growing gradually cooler for the past three decades."

In 1974 the National Science Board, the governing body of the National Science Foundation, stated: "During the last 20 to 30 years, world temperature has fallen, irregularly at first but more sharply over the last decade." Two years earlier, the board had observed: "Judging from the record of the past interglacial ages, the present time of high temperatures should be drawing to an end . . . leading into the next glacial age."

No wonder the late political scientist Aaron Wildavsky called global warming alarmism the 'mother of all environmental scares.'

How quickly things change. Fear of the coming ice age is old hat, but fear that man-made greenhouse gases are causing temperatures to rise to harmful levels is in vogue. Alarmists brazenly assert that this phenomenon is fact, and that the science of climate change is "settled."

Sound Empirical Science
Challenges Alarmists

Today, even saying there is scientific disagreement over global warming is itself controversial. But anyone who pays even cursory attention to the issue understands that scientists vigorously disagree over whether human activities are responsible for global warming, or whether those activities will precipitate natural disasters.

I would submit, furthermore, that not only is there a debate, but the debate is shifting away from those who subscribe to global warming alarmism. After studying the issue over the last several years, I believe that the balance of the evidence offers strong proof that natural variability is the overwhelming factor influencing climate.

Thus far no one has seriously demonstrated any scientific proof that increased global temperatures would lead to the catastrophes predicted by alarmists.

It's also important to question whether global warming is even a problem for human existence. Thus far no one has seriously demonstrated any scientific proof that increased global temperatures would lead to the catastrophes predicted by alarmists. In fact, it appears that just the opposite is true: that increases in global temperatures may have a beneficial effect on how we live our lives.

For these reasons I would like to discuss an important body of scientific research that refutes the anthropogenic theory of catastrophic global warming. I believe this research offers compelling proof that human activities have little impact on climate.

This research, well documented in the scientific literature, directly challenges the environmental worldview of the media, so they typically don't receive proper attention and discussion. Certain members of the media would rather level personal attacks on scientists who question "accepted" global warming theories than engage on the science.

I believe it is extremely important for the future of this country that the facts and the science get a fair hearing. Without proper knowledge and understanding, alarmists will scare the country into enacting its ultimate goal: making energy suppression, in the form of harmful mandatory restrictions on carbon dioxide and other greenhouse emissions, the official policy of the United States.

Such a policy [of restricting greenhouse gas emissions] would induce serious economic harm, especially for low-income and minority populations.

Such a policy would induce serious economic harm, especially for low-income and minority populations. Energy suppression, as official government and non-partisan private analyses have amply confirmed, means higher prices for food, medical care, and electricity, as well as massive job losses and drastic reductions in gross domestic product, all the while providing virtually no environmental benefit. In other words: a raw deal for the American people and a crisis for the poor.

Kyoto Treaty Would Wreck Economy

The issue of global warming has garnered significant international attention through the Kyoto Treaty, which requires signatories to reduce their greenhouse gas emissions by considerable amounts below 1990 levels.

The Clinton Administration, led by former Vice President Al Gore, signed Kyoto on November 12, 1998, but never submitted it to the Senate for ratification.

The treaty explicitly acknowledges as true that man-made emissions, principally from the use of fossil fuels, are causing global temperatures to rise, eventually to catastrophic levels. Kyoto enthusiasts believe that if we dramatically cut back, or even eliminate, fossil fuels, the climate system will respond by sending global temperatures back to "normal" levels.

In 1997, the Senate sent a powerful signal that Kyoto was unacceptable. By a vote of 95 to 0, the Senate passed the Byrd-Hagel resolution, which stated that the Senate would not ratify Kyoto if it caused substantial economic harm and if developing countries were not required to participate on the same timetable. . . .

The Congressional Budget Office (CBO) provided further proof that Kyoto-like carbon regulatory schemes are regressive and harmful to economic growth and prosperity.

In July, the Congressional Budget Office (CBO) provided further proof that Kyoto-like carbon regulatory schemes are regressive and harmful to economic growth and prosperity.

As the CBO found, "The price increases resulting from a carbon cap would be regressive—that is, they would place a relatively greater burden on lower-income households than on higher-income ones."

Despite these facts, [environmental] groups such as Greenpeace blindly assert that Kyoto "will not impose significant costs" and "will not be an economic burden."

Among the many questions this provokes, one might ask: Won't be a burden on whom, exactly?

Greenpeace doesn't elaborate, but according to a recent study by the Center for Energy and Economic Development, sponsored by the National Black Chamber of Commerce and the United States Hispanic Chamber of Commerce, if the U.S. ratifies Kyoto, or passes domestic climate policies effectively implementing the treaty, the result would "disproportionately harm America's minority communities, and place the economic advancement of millions of U.S. blacks and Hispanics at risk."

Among the study's key findings: Kyoto will cost 511,000 jobs held by Hispanic workers and 864,000 jobs held by black workers; poverty rates for minority families will increase dramatically; and, because Kyoto will bring about higher energy prices, many minority businesses will be lost.

Environmental alarmists, as a matter of faith, peddle the notion that climate change is, as Greenpeace put it, 'the biggest environmental threat facing . . . developing countries.

Environmental alarmists, as an article of faith, peddle the notion that climate change is, as Greenpeace put it, "the biggest environmental threat facing . . . developing countries." For one, such thinking runs contrary to the public declaration of the 2002 World Summit on Sustainable Development—a program sponsored by the United Nations—which found that poverty is the No. 1 threat facing developing countries.

Some in this body have introduced Kyoto-like legislation that would hurt low-income and minority populations. Last year [2002], Tom Mullen, president of Cleveland Catholic Charities, testified [before the Senate] against S. 556, the Clean Power Act, which would impose onerous, unrealistic restrictions, including a Kyoto-like cap on carbon dioxide emissions, on electric utilities. He noted that this regime would mean higher electricity prices for the poorest citizens of Cleveland.

For those on fixed incomes, as Mr. Mullen pointed out, higher electricity prices present a choice between eating and staying warm in winter or cool in summer. As Mr. Mullen said, "The overall impact on the economy in Northeast Ohio would be overwhelming, and the needs that we address at Catholic Charities in Ohio with the elderly and poor would be well beyond our capacity and that of our current partners in government and the private sector."[1]

In addition to its negative economic impacts, Kyoto still does not satisfy Byrd-Hagel's concerns about developing countries. Though such countries as China, India, Brazil, South Korea, and Mexico are signatories to Kyoto, they are not required to reduce their emissions, even though they emit nearly 30 percent of the world's greenhouse gases. And within a generation they will be the world's largest emitters of carbon, methane and other such greenhouse gases.

Despite the fact that neither of Byrd-Hagel's conditions has been met, environmentalists have bitterly criticized President Bush for abandoning Kyoto. But one wonders: why don't they assail the 95 senators, both Democrats and Republicans, who, according to Byrd-Hagel, oppose Kyoto as it stands today, and who would, presumably, oppose ratification if the treaty came up on the Senate floor?

And why don't they assail former President Clinton, or former Vice President Gore, who signed the treaty but never submitted it to the Senate for ratification?

To repeat, it was the unanimous vote of this body that Kyoto was and still is unacceptable. Several of my colleagues who believe that humans are responsible for global warming, including Sen. Jeffords (I.-Vt.), Sen. Kennedy (D.-Mass.), Sen. Boxer (D.-Calif.), former Sen. Moseley-Braun (D.-Ill.), Sen. Lieberman (D.-Conn.), and Sen. Kerry (D.-Mass.), all voted for Byrd-Hagel.

1. This bill had not been passed at the time of publication.

Again, all of these senators, the most outspoken proponents of Kyoto, voted in favor of Byrd-Hagel.

Remember, Byrd-Hagel said the Senate would not ratify
Kyoto if it caused substantial economic harm and if developing countries were not required to participate on the same
timetable. So, if the Byrd-Hagel conditions are ever satisfied,
should the United States ratify Kyoto?

Answering that question depends on several factors, including whether Kyoto would provide significant, needed environmental benefits.

The Kyoto Protocol Would Accomplish Nothing

First, we should ask what Kyoto is designed to accomplish. According to the UN's Intergovernmental Panel on Climate
Change (IPCC), Kyoto will achieve "stabilization of greenhouse gas concentrations in the atmosphere at a level that
would prevent dangerous anthropogenic interference with the
climate system."

What does this statement mean? The IPCC offers no elabo-
ration and doesn't provide any scientific explanation about
what that level would be. Why? The answer is simple: thus far
no one has found a definitive scientific answer.

Dr. S. Fred Singer, an atmospheric scientist at the University of Virginia, who served as the first Director of the U.S.
Weather Satellite Service (which is now in the Department of
Commerce) and more recently as a member and vice chairman of the National Advisory Committee on Oceans and Atmosphere (NACOA), said that "No one knows what constitutes a 'dangerous' concentration. There exists, as yet, no
scientific basis for defining such a concentration, or even of
knowing whether it is more or less than current levels of carbon dioxide."

One might pose the question: if we had the ability to set
the global thermostat, what temperature would we pick?

Would we set it colder or warmer than it is today? What would the optimal temperature be? The actual dawn of civilization occurred in a period climatologists call the "climatic optimum" when the mean surface temperature was 1–2 degrees Celsius warmer than today. Why not go 1 to 2 degrees Celsius higher? Or 1 to 2 degrees lower for that matter?

The Kyoto emissions reduction targets are arbitrary, lacking in any real scientific basis. Kyoto therefore will have virtually no impact on global temperatures. This is not just my opinion, but the conclusion reached by the country's top climate scientists.

One might pose the question: if we had the ability to set the global thermostat, what temperature would we pick?

Dr. Tom Wigley, a senior scientist at the National Center for Atmospheric Research, found that if the Kyoto Protocol were fully implemented by all signatories—now I will note here that this next point assumes that the alarmists' science is correct, which of course it is not—if Kyoto were fully implemented it would reduce temperatures by a mere 0.07 degrees Celsius by 2050, and 0.13 degrees Celsius by 2100. What does this mean? Such an amount is so small that ground-based thermometers cannot reliably measure it.

Dr. Richard Lindzen, an MIT [Massachusetts Institute of Technology] scientist and member of the National Academy of Sciences, who has specialized in climate issues for over 30 years, told the Committee on Environment and Public Works on May 2, 2001 that there is a "definitive disconnect between Kyoto and science. Should a catastrophic scenario prove correct, Kyoto would not prevent it."

Similarly, Dr. James Hansen of NASA [National Aeronautics and Space Administration], considered the father of global warming theory, said that Kyoto Protocol "will have little effect" on global temperature in the 21st century. In a rather stunning follow-up, Hansen said it would take *30 Kyotos*—let me repeat that—*30 Kyotos* to reduce warming to an acceptable level. If one Kyoto devastates the American economy, what would 30 do?

So this leads to another question: if the provisions in the Protocol do little or nothing measurable to influence global temperatures, what does this tell us about the scientific basis of Kyoto?

Answering that question requires a thorough examination of the scientific work conducted by the U.N.'s Intergovernmental Panel on Climate Change, which provides the scientific basis for Kyoto, international climate negotiations, and the substance of claims made by alarmists.

IPCC Assessment Reports

In 1992, several nations from around the globe gathered in Rio de Janeiro for the United Nations Framework Convention on Climate Change. The meeting was premised on the concern that global warming was becoming a problem. The U.S., along with many others, signed the Framework Convention, committing them to making voluntary reductions in greenhouse gases.

Over time, it became clear that signatories were not achieving their reduction targets as stipulated under Rio. This realization led to the Kyoto Protocol in 1997, which was an amendment to the Framework Convention, and which prescribed mandatory reductions only for developed nations. [By the way, leaving out developing nations was an explicit violation of Byrd-Hagel.]

The science of Kyoto is based on the "Assessment Reports" conducted by the Intergovernmental Panel on Climate Change, or IPCC. Over the last 13 years, the IPCC has published three assessments, with each one over time growing more and more alarmist.

The first IPCC Assessment report in 1990 found that the climate record of the past century was "broadly consistent" with the changes in Earth's surface temperature, as calculated by climate models that incorporated the observed increase in greenhouse gases.

This conclusion, however, appears suspect considering the climate cooled between 1940 and 1975, just as industrial activity grew rapidly after World War II. It has been difficult to reconcile this cooling with the observed increase in greenhouse gases.

After its initial publication, the IPCC's Second Assessment report in 1995 attracted widespread international attention, particularly among scientists who believed that human activities were causing global warming. In their view, the report provided the proverbial smoking gun.

The most widely cited phrase from the report—actually, it came from the report summary, as few in the media actually read the entire report—was that "the balance of the evidence suggests a discernible human influence on global climate." This of course is so vague that it's essentially meaningless.

What do they mean by "suggests?" And, for that matter, what, in this particular context, does "discernible" mean? How much human influence is discernible? Is it a positive or negative influence? Where is the precise scientific quantification? Unfortunately the media created the impression that man-induced global warming was fact. On August 10, 1995, the *New York Times* published an article titled "Experts Confirm Human Role in Global Warming." According to the *Times'* account, the IPCC showed that global warming "is unlikely to be entirely due to natural causes."

Of course, when parsed, this account means fairly little. Not entirely due to natural causes? Well, how much, then? 1%? 20%? 85%?

The IPCC report was replete with caveats and qualifications, providing little evidence to support anthropogenic theories of global warming. The preceding paragraph in which the "balance of evidence" quote appears makes exactly that point.

Moreover, the IPCC report was quite explicit about the uncertainties surrounding a link between human actions and global warming. "Although these global mean results suggest that there is some anthropogenic component in the observed temperature record, *they cannot be considered compelling evidence* of a clear cause-and-effect link between anthropogenic forcing and changes in the Earth's surface temperature."

Remember, the IPCC provides the scientific basis for the alarmists' conclusions about global warming. But even the IPCC is saying that their own science cannot be considered compelling evidence.

IPCC's Third Report Is Heavily Politicized

Five years later, the IPCC was back again, this time with the Third Assessment Report on Climate Change. In October of 2000, the IPCC *Summary for Policymakers* was leaked to the media, which once again accepted the IPCC's conclusions as fact.

Based on the summary, the *Washington Post* wrote on October 30, "The consensus on global warming keeps strengthening." In a similar vein, the *New York Times* confidently declared on October 28, "The international panel of climate scientists, considered the most authoritative voice on global warming, has now concluded that mankind's contribution to the problem is greater than originally believed."

Note again, look at how these accounts are couched: they are worded to maximize the fear factor. But upon closer inspection, it's clear that such statements have no compelling intellectual content. "Greater than originally believed?" What is the baseline from which the *Times* makes such a judgment? Is it .01%, or 25%? And how much is greater? Double? Triple? An order of magnitude greater?

Such reporting prompted testimony by Dr. Richard Lindzen before the Committee on Environment and Public Works, the committee I now chair, in May of 2001. Lindzen said, "Nearly all reading and coverage of the IPCC is restricted to the highly publicized Summaries for Policymakers, which are written by representatives from governments, NGOs [non-governmental organizations] and business; the full reports, written by participating scientists, are largely ignored."

As it turned out, the Policymaker's Summary was politicized and radically differed from an earlier draft. . . . The final version looks quite different, and concluded instead: "In the light of new evidence and taking into account the remaining uncertainties, most of the observed warming over the last 50 years is likely to have been due to the increase in greenhouse gas concentrations."

In short, some parts of the IPCC process resembled a Soviet-style trial, in which the facts are predetermined, and ideological purity trumps technical and scientific rigor.

The predictions in the summary went far beyond those in the IPCC's 1995 report. In the Second Assessment, the IPCC predicted that the earth could warm by 1 to 3.5 degrees Celsius by the year 2100. The "best estimate" was a 2-degree-Celsius warming by 2100. Both are highly questionable at best.

In the Third Assessment, the IPCC dramatically increased that estimate to a range of 1.4 to 5.8 degrees Celsius, even though no new evidence had come to light to justify such a dramatic change.

In fact, the IPCC's median projected warming actually declined from 1990 to 1995. The IPCC 1990 initial estimate was 3.2°C, then the IPCC revised 1992 estimate was 2.6°C, followed by the IPCC revised 1995 estimate of 2.0°C.

What changed? As it turned out, the new prediction was based on faulty, politically charged assumptions about trends in population growth, economic growth, and fossil fuel use.

The extreme-case scenario of a 5.8-degree warming, for instance, rests on an assumption that the whole world will raise its level of economic activity and per capita energy use to that of the United States, and that energy use will be carbon intensive. This scenario is simply ludicrous. This essentially contradicts the experience of the industrialized world over the last 30 years. Yet the 5.8-degree figure featured prominently in news stories because it produced the biggest fear effect.

In short, these general circulation models, or GCMs as they're known, create simulations that must track over 5 million parameters. These simulations require accurate information on two natural greenhouse gas factors—water vapor and clouds—whose effects scientists still do not understand.

Again, to reiterate in plain English, this means the models do not account for key variables that influence the climate system.

Despite this, the alarmists continue to use these models and all the other flimsy evidence I've cited to support their theories of man-made global warming.

Global Warming Is Not Caused by Human Activities

William M. Gray

About the author: William M. Gray is a professor at Colorado State University in the Department of Atmospheric Science.

By the end of the 21st century the concentration of greenhouse gases from human activity in Earth's atmosphere is expected to double from preindustrial values. Many believe this increase will cause a 2 to 5 degree Celsius (3.6 to 9 degrees Fahrenheit) increase in Earth's temperature. These projections are based largely on government-sponsored U.S. and foreign Global Computer Model simulations.

These computer models use a number of complicated mathematical formulas to simulate the physical processes of the atmosphere and ocean circulation. They forecast future changes in the atmosphere and ocean by simultaneously solving an array of equations that are envisaged to represent the real physical processes of the Earth's climate system. There is some imprecision in the accuracy of these equations with regard to their ability to represent the real atmosphere. Time steps vary from about 15 minutes to an hour or so. They integrate this set of simultaneous equations for hundreds of thousands of time steps into the future. Separate calculations are made, which include and exclude the human-induced greenhouse gas inputs of carbon dioxide and methane. Though these models have become more sophisticated over the past few decades, the methodology appears to be compromised by two basic flaws.

Flawed Models

First, the models assume that more rainfall, resulting from the buildup of greenhouse gases, will lead to significant increases

William M. Gray, "The Errors of Chicken Little Thinking," *Forum for Applied Research and Public Policy*, vol. 16, summer 2002. Copyright © 2002 by The University of Tennessee, EERC. Reproduced by permission.

in atmospheric water vapor, especially in the upper atmosphere, and in cirrus cloudiness. These increases are presumed to significantly reduce the radiation energy sent back to space. To compensate for this assumed reduction in outgoing radiation to space, the globe must warm so that it can compensate for this reduced energy flux. Energy to space increases with global temperature. Observations and theoretical analysis by myself and others, however, suggest that reductions in outgoing radiation, due to increases in global rainfall, will be very small, and will not cause significant global warming.

A second flaw in the Global Computer Model simulations is their inability to make realistic simulations of ocean circulation processes many decades into the future. Since about 70 percent of the atmosphere is in contact with the ocean surface, ocean circulation patterns are fundamental to climate variability.

Water Vapor

The primary greenhouse gas in the atmosphere, by far, is water vapor. It is the influence of the human-caused greenhouse gases, such as carbon dioxide and methane, on water vapor that is most in question. If the addition of human-induced greenhouse gases leads to an enhancement of water vapor's dominant influence (a positive feedback), then humans will, indeed, be responsible for significant warming. But it is more likely that the human-induced gases will act as a modulator (negative feedback) of water vapor's influence. If the human-induced greenhouse gases will act to slightly reduce water vapor's influence as a greenhouse gas, then little global warming will result.

Most researchers agree that the Earth will rid itself of most of the positive energy gains from human-induced greenhouse gas by developing extra surface evaporation and compensating extra global rainfall, which has a cooling effect on the Earth's surface. The key question is how the atmosphere will respond to this expected increase in global evaporation rainfall. Will the expected increase in human-induced greenhouse gases cause a positive, a neutral, or a negative trend in net global outgoing radiation? The Global Computer Models are programmed to give large—and apparently unrealistic—reductions in outgoing radiation to space as global rainfall increases.

If the human-induced greenhouse gases will act to slightly reduce water vapor's influence as a greenhouse gas, then little global warming will result.

The runaway global warming scenarios predicted by current Global Computer Model technology grossly overestimate the actual threat. As more-realistic computer simulations become available in the future, I believe we will learn that the runaway global warming scenarios predicted by current Global Computer Model technology grossly overestimate the actual threat, and that the small surface warming trends observed in global surface temperature during the last 25 to 100 years, which have been so highly touted in the press, are primarily of natural origin and not due to human influences. And, of course, we can do little or nothing about natural climate change.

Give Me Feedback

Most geophysical systems react to forced imbalances by developing reactions that oppose and weaken the initial imbalance; hence, there is a negative feedback response. Recent global scenarios spawned by Global Computer Model climate simulations, however, hypothesize a large positive feedback effect. Thus, projected human-induced greenhouse gas increases have been programmed into these models as a strong enhancing mechanism for global warming beyond what would be accomplished by anthropogenic gases themselves. Specifically, these models have built-in assumptions that, as human-induced greenhouse gases increase, water vapor and cloud concentrations in the upper atmosphere will increase, causing a significant amount of extra outgoing radiation, which would normally be emitted to space, to be trapped within the atmosphere, thus, resulting in additional warming.

The runaway global warming scenarios predicted by current Global Computer Model technology grossly overestimate the actual threat.

The Global Computer Model simulations have been programmed to give a reduction in global outgoing long-wave radiation energy to space that is five to 10 times greater than the reductions that would occur from the human-induced greenhouse gas increases alone. That is why most of these Global Computer Models develop a 2-to-5-degree Celsius global warming, for a doubling of human-induced greenhouse gases. Such large, assumed positive, human-induced greenhouse gas feedbacks are unrealistic and atypical of how most geophysical systems function.

A doubling of human-induced greenhouse gases will bring about only minor amounts of global warming. Instead, if atmospheric upper-level water vapor and cirrus cloudiness were constant, or were slightly reduced—for a doubling of human-induced greenhouse gases—only a small global warming of less than 0.2 to 0.3 degrees Celsius would occur. A doubling of human-induced greenhouse gases will bring about only minor amounts of global warming, and global agreements, such as the Kyoto Treaty, to reduce such gases would have little effect and would not be economically justified.

Global Rainfall

A doubling of human-induced greenhouse gases will likely cause only a small ... temperature increase of less than 0.3 [degrees] Celsius. Most researchers agree that increased amounts of greenhouse gases will lead to an increase in global rainfall. It is unlikely, however, that this expected increase in global rainfall will bring about a large positive increase in the reduction of radiation energy to space, despite what the Global Computer Models suggest. Rather, increases in human-induced greenhouse gases will more likely bring about a weak negative, or at best neutral, response with regard to changes in upper level water vapor and cirrus cloudiness. This would lead to a weak negative, not a positive response, of upper level water vapor and cirrus to global rainfall increase. This negative feedback influence would lead to a small increase, not a decrease, of net radiation energy to space. Such a negative response would cancel most of the greenhouse gas warming anticipated by the much touted Global Computer Model simulations. A doubling of human-induced greenhouse gases will likely cause only a small positive global surface temperature increase of less than 0.3 [degrees] Celsius.

I do not believe that the Global Computer Model computer warming scenarios are a realistic response to a doubling of human-induced greenhouse gases (most give roughly similar warming values). It is more likely that this gas doubling, and a consequent 3-to-4 percent increase in global rainfall, will lead to only a small increase—not a decrease—in net radiation loss to space. Such a response should bring about only negligible increases in global surface temperature.

Evidence

Various observational and theoretical speculations suggest that the enhancement of global precipitation, in response to human-induced greenhouse gas increases, will not cause a significant decrease in the net outgoing radiation to space. This evidence includes:

- Diurnal variations. Any changes in the global hydrological cycle, including diurnal rainfall, temperature, and vertical motion changes, affect the amount of atmospheric water vapor and cirrus clouds and, ultimately, the amount of outgoing radiation to space. By studying the diurnal variation of cumulus convection over the tropical oceans, we find twice as much deep convection and heavy rainfall in the morning as in the late afternoon and evening. Rainfall is heaviest during the early-morning hours. It is at this time that outgoing long-wave radiation to space is the greatest. There is, thus, not a direct (but an inverse) relationship between heavy rainfall and radiation loss to space.

• Hurricanes and typhoons. Hurricanes and typhoons, and their environments from their centers out to 1,000 km, typically have more net rainfall per unit area than the nonstorm regions, but also have more radiation loss to space than do nonstorm areas. This is also indicative of an inverse rainfall-radiation loss response.

• Upper level water vapor. Tropical west Pacific Ocean surface temperatures have increased between 1975 and 2000 as overall sea surface temperature values in this region increased. But upper level water vapor content did not increase. This trend indicates that surface warming over the tropical oceans is linked more to upper level drying than to upper level moistening. Such upper drying leads to larger outgoing radiation to space.

• Sea surface temperature. Were oceanic surface temperature to rise, the areas of cloudiness and areas of increased rainfall from tropical convection would decrease. This should be expected to also lead to an increase in outgoing radiation and a slight cooling of the Earth-atmosphere system.

• Satellite and balloon observations. During the past 20 to 40 years, satellite and balloon observations of temperatures in the troposphere do not show a significant increase, as was predicted by the Global Computer Model scenarios. Analyses of global tropospheric temperature trends, from satellites since 1979 and from weather balloons since 1958, show no significant warming trends. These measurements do not agree with most of the general climate model results, which predict that a global warming of 0.3 to 0.5 degree Celsius should have resulted from the increased greenhouse gas concentrations since the late 1950s. Modelers have speculated that these recent differences between observation and Global Computer Model temperature predictions have been caused by industrial aerosols, such as sulfates, emitted in the Northern Hemisphere. These aerosols were not incorporated into the earlier simulations. The aerosols, however, cannot explain all such predicted and observed temperature differences. It is likely that the failure to deal properly with water vapor feedback—not the lack of incorporation of sulfates—is the primary cause of these observed-versus-model forecast discrepancies.

Devil in the Details

General-circulation models contain other flaws. For example, they aren't very good at modeling details of the distribution of water vapor in space and time. They also do not adequately simulate the diurnal variation of air masses that rise and fall with daily temperature fluctuations.

About half of the global rainfall at any time occurs in concentrated areas of but a few kilometers wide and over time periods of less than an hour. These heavy rainfall areas in aggregate cover only about 0.25 to 1 percent of the Earth's surface but can have significant effects on the hydrologic cycle. The grid scales of Global Computer Model simulations are much larger than the size of the individual heavy rainfall events. There is no hope of directly modeling such heavy rainfall concentrations. Yet, to properly model the influence of the hydrologic cycle, the effects of these small, horizontal scale, heavy rainfall features with their strong downdraft drying influences must be realistically accommodated.

This need for including accurate small-grid-scale convection parameters appears to be a fundamental modeling deficiency. This has led to the need to parameterize these small and intense cumulus events in terms of the larger scales of motion. Many modelers are unfamiliar with the complicated and detailed functioning of the hydrologic cycle, and they consequently have not been able to realistically incorporate these processes into their global model simulations. Modelers have tended to avoid facing up to this difficult task of coming to grips with the problems of realistic simulation of the hydrologic cycle. This has been a big factor in their generation of unrealistic warming scenarios. Faulty understanding and poor resolution of these sub-grid scale convective events, which are then integrated hundreds of thousands of time steps into the future guarantee unrealistic simulations and a lack of confidence in the results.

Though we should continue research into global warming, we should not implement global fossil-fuel restrictions on the basis of what we know now. General-circulation model simulations by large government laboratories, on which most of the global warming scenarios are based, thus have basic flaws. If the models can't skillfully predict next fall's or next winter's temperature trends, or even make accurate hindcasts of last fall's or last winter's temperature, why should we trust them to make accurate predictions 50 to 100 years down the road?

Hydrologic Thermostat

The long-term stability of global temperature—despite variations of ice ages, vegetation, and ocean currents, to name a few—requires that the Earth's system has built-in regulating mechanisms. The hydrologic cycle appears to be one of these regulatory mechanisms. When the Earth's surface experiences an anomalous gain of energy, it responds by balancing much of this excess energy through enhanced evaporation and a stronger hydrologic cycle of more concentrated rainfall. Increased rainfall leads to a small decrease in atmospheric water vapor and cirrus cloudiness. This causes an enhancement of net outgoing long-wave radiation. Such changes act to balance out most of such anomalous energy gain.

Though we should continue research into global warming, we should not implement global fossil-fuel restrictions on the basis of what we know now.

By contrast, when the Earth's surface cools, as it did during the ice ages, the hydrologic cycle weakens. Decreased rainfall and increased upper-level water-vapor changes act to balance the energy deficit by suppressing some of the radiation energy lost to space. These balancing hydrologic cycle changes allow the Earth to oppose and help accommodate externally and internally forced energy differences. Such negative feedbacks are an important process that keeps the global surface energy budget in a general balance despite positive or negative forces that would drive it out of balance. The hydrologic cycle itself acts as one of these ameliorating feedback mechanisms.

We conclude . . . that global warming from a doubling of greenhouse gases will actually be quite modest. It is not possible at present to make a precise quantitative assessment of just how much atmospheric water vapor and cirrus cloudiness will change if human-induced greenhouse gases double. But we can say that they will be different than the changes occurring in the current simulations. We conclude, therefore, that global warming from a doubling of greenhouse gases will actually be quite modest. . . .

Exaggerations

Unfortunately, there has not yet been an open and objective scientific dialogue on this topic. The human-induced global warming scenarios that have been so much in the headlines since the hot summer of 1988 have been grossly exaggerated by a broad spectrum of scientists who, although competent in their own specialties, know little about the processes of the hydrologic cycle and how the global atmosphere and oceans really function.

Many of my more experienced colleagues and I have invested decades of our lives in the study of how the atmosphere functions. We have been appalled by the many alarmist statements issued by high-ranking government officials, particularly during the Clinton administration, and by prominent scientists who have so little real understanding of climate change. Their views have been shaped by selective sources, in particular the environmental and large Global Computer Model groups who have a vested interest in promoting the warming threat.

Global temperatures have always fluctuated back and forth and will continue to do so regardless of the amount of human-induced greenhouse gases that are released into the atmosphere. Although initially generated by honest questions of how human-produced greenhouse gases might affect global climate, this topic has now taken on a life of its own that has been grossly exaggerated by those hoping to exploit the ignorance of the general public on climate matters. These include groups in our federal government, the media, and scientists who are willing to bend their objectivity to obtain government research grants for global warming studies.

Humans Cannot Prevent Climate Change

Those who stress the importance of human-induced global warming are irresponsible to interpret nearly every instance of unusual weather as likely evidence of a human impact. It is surprising that more atmospheric scientists have not spoken out about the reliability of the Global Computer Model simulations and their overly simplified arguments. Our government, the media, and many nonclimate-trained scientists have been irresponsible to suggest that so many of the extreme weather events in recent years likely have a human-induced greenhouse gas component. Extreme weather events occurred even before humans began emitting tons of carbon dioxide and other greenhouse gases into the atmosphere. With all the human problems facing the world—such as poverty, famine, disease, overpopulation, terrorism, crime, drugs, and AIDS—it is irresponsible to imply that human-induced global warming is one of the major threats facing mankind.

Those who stress the importance of human-induced global warming are irresponsible to interpret nearly every instance of unusual weather as likely evidence of a human impact.

There is little or nothing humans can do to prevent natural climate change; we must adapt to any future climate changes. Restricting human-induced greenhouse gas emissions now, on the basis of their assumed influence on global warming, is not a viable economic option, even if it were politically possible. I am convinced that in 15 to 20 years, we will look back on this period of global warming hysteria as we now look back on so many other popular, and trendy, scientific ideas—such as the generally accepted eugenics theories of the 1920s and 1930s that have now been discredited. I agree with a statement made in June 2001 by Richard Lindzen of the Massachusetts Institute of Technology that "Science, in the public arena, is commonly used as a source of authority with which to bludgeon political opponents and propagandize un-informed citizens. . . . It is a reprehensible practice that cor-rodes our ability to make rational decisions."

CHAPTER 3

How Can the Government Best Conserve the Environment?

Chapter Preface

One way the government can help conserve the environment is to purchase environmentally friendly products. The U.S government is one of the largest purchasers in America. In fact, the nation's eighty-seven thousand federal, state, and local governments spend roughly $385 billion a year on goods and services. From cars to office supplies to energy, government purchases make up around 18 percent of the total gross domestic product. As the single largest purchasing entity, the U.S. government has the buying power to affect the environment in positive ways.

The government has embraced this role by participating in Environmental Preferable Purchasing. When considering what products to purchase, the government examines the environmental performance of "green" goods and services in comparison to the performance and cost of traditional products. Some of the qualities that are considered when evaluating eco-friendly products are durability, recycled content, energy efficiency, and safer manufacturing approaches. For example, one way the government can reduce energy waste is by purchasing computers that are Energy Star compliant—meaning they have been rated to be highly energy efficient. According to Brian Johnson, the manager of Santa Monica, California's environmental programs division, it's easy for government entities to purchase green. He notes, "Green procurement provides cost savings, is easily implementable, and enhances public health and the environment. Some of these purchases are simply no-brainers. If you have a choice between a carcinogenic bathroom cleaner and one that isn't, I can't imagine not choosing the safer alternative."

There are many eco-friendly products on the market, but they face tough competition from mainstream brands that are often cheaper and more well-known. However, if the government sets an example by purchasing green products, others will follow. Green procurement has been especially successful with recycled paper. In 1992 President Bill Clinton signed an executive order requiring that all government agencies buy recycled paper despite complaints about price, preference, and availability. Ten years later, 98 percent of paper purchased by the federal government contained at least 30 percent of post-consumer materials. Many state and local governments have followed the U.S. government's lead because if they use federal funds they must abide by federal purchasing standards. Since individuals work at these agencies, they too become exposed to eco-friendly buying trends and are more aware of the alternative products available for purchase in their private lives.

While government green purchasing sounds like a relatively easy solution to environmental problems, it has not been easy to implement and enforce. President Jimmy Carter created the Resource and Conservation Recovery Act in 1976 to encourage the government's purchase and use of recycled paper, but the program met with limited success. In the sixteen years that the law existed prior to Clinton's executive order, only 12 percent of the U.S. government's paper purchase complied with the act. Some critics feel that many environmental laws are designed as good publicity more than as good environmental policy. Mike Shore, a spokesperson for Green Seal, an environmental product certifier, comments, "While there is firm policy in the federal government to consider the environment both in laws and regulations by the OMB [Office of Management and Budget], and while there are people in the trenches who want to carry them out, there is very little information available to them, thanks partly to the bureaucratic sludge and partly to the lack of interest of the EPA [Environmental Protection Agency] in advancing the program it's chartered to carry out."

The debate continues over how the federal government should strengthen its green purchasing program. Its success or failure will have an enormous impact on other purchasers, and in turn, the environment.

The Clear Skies Act Will Reduce Pollution

The White House

About the author: The White House is the central office representing the executive branch of the United States government. Its Web site provides daily news releases about important matters concerning public policy and summations of the president's speeches and actions.

Today [February 14, 2002], President [George W.] Bush proposed the most significant step America has ever taken to cut power plant emissions, the Clear Skies Initiative. This new proposal will aggressively reduce air pollution from electricity generators and improve air quality throughout the country. The Clear Skies Initiative will cut air pollution 70 percent, using a proven, market-based approach that will save American consumers millions of dollars.

America needs a clean, secure, affordable, reliable energy supply in the years ahead. President Bush has often said that environmental protection and energy production are not competing priorities. This progressive plan shows how that objective can be reached. We can meet our environmental goals while providing affordable electricity for American consumers and American businesses.

America has made great progress in reducing air pollution. Over the last three decades, air pollution has declined by 29 percent, while our economy has grown nearly 160 percent. These gains have provided cleaner air for millions of people. Our understanding of science, technology, and markets has improved since the Clean Air Act was passed in 1970. We know more about the best way to reduce pollution, and how

The White House, "Executive Summary: The Clear Skies Initiative," www.whitehouse-.gov, February 14, 2002.

to do it cost effectively. The acid rain cap and trade program created by Congress in 1990 reduced more pollution in the last decade than all other Clean Air Act command-and-control programs[1] combined, and achieved significant reductions at two-thirds of the cost to accomplish those reductions using a "command-and-control" system. It's time to take the best of what we have learned and modernize the Clean Air Act. That's why President Bush is proposing a new Clean Air Act for the 21st century.

The Goals of the Clear Skies Initiative

The Clear Skies Initiative will:

Dramatically Cut Power Plants' Emissions of Three of the Worst Air Pollutants.

- Cut sulfur dioxide (SO_2) emissions by 73 percent, from current emissions of 11 million tons to a cap of 4.5 million tons in 2010, and 3 million tons in 2018.

- Cut emissions of nitrogen oxides (NO_x) by 67 percent, from current emissions of 5 million tons to a cap of 2.1 million tons in 2008, and to 1.7 million tons in 2018.

- Cutting mercury emissions by 69 percent—the first-ever national cap on mercury emissions. Emissions will be cut from current emissions of 48 tons to a cap of 26 tons in 2010, and 15 tons in 2018.

- Emission caps will be set to account for different air quality needs in the East and the West.

Use a New, Market-Based Approach to Clean Air :

- Protect Americans from respiratory and cardiovascular diseases by dramatically reducing smog, fine particulate

1. Cap and Trade programs establish cap limits on pollutants and offer companies or groups economic incentives for reducing their emissions by allowing them to sell their limits to companies that have exceeded their pollutant emissions. Command-and-control programs use institutional regulation that bans or limits the discharge of certain pollutants and does not allow benefits for not meeting those limits.

matter, regional haze; and protect wildlife habitat and ecosystem health from acid rain, nitrogen and mercury deposition. NO_x and SO_2 emissions both contribute to fine particulate matter emissions and NO_x also contributes to ground-level ozone or smog.

- Save Americans as much as $1 billion annually in compliance costs that are passed along to American consumers, while improving air quality and protecting the reliability and affordability of electricity for consumers.

- Cut pollution further, faster, cheaper—and with more certainty—eliminating the need for expensive and uncertain litigation as a means of achieving clean air.

- Build upon the 1990 Clean Air Act's acid rain program, America's most successful clean air law in the last decade, and encourage the use of new pollution control technologies.

President Bush has a strong track record on enacting far-reaching clean air initiatives. In 1999, then-Governor Bush signed legislation that permanently caps NO_x and SO_2 emissions from older power plants in Texas starting in 2003. The legislation was widely hailed as a model for the country. The Texas program is designed to reduce NO_x emissions by 75,000 tons per year, and SO_2 emissions by 35,000 tons per year, while giving utilities flexibility in determining how and where to achieve the reductions....

The Success of the Clean Air Act

In the U.S., power plants emit significant amounts of air pollution: 67 percent of all sulfur dioxide (SO_2) emissions, 37 percent of mercury emissions, and 25 percent of all nitrogen oxide (NO_x) emissions. These pollutants contribute to a variety of health and environmental problems, such as smog, acid rain, nitrogen deposition and visibility impairment.

Current law addresses each of these pollutants independently, on different timetables, through several different programs. These laws are uncoordinated and often inconsistent. Power plants might install equipment one year that is rendered obsolete the next. Implementation and enforcement usually requires years of litigation, leaving the fate of America's air to the uncertainties of the courtroom.

After 30 years of experience in regulating air pollution, America has proved that there is a better way to accomplish our clean air goals.

After 30 years of experience in regulating air pollution, America has proved that there is a better way to accomplish our clean air goals.

The 1990 Clean Air Act Amendments, proposed and signed into law by President George H.W. Bush, have significantly reduced air pollution, especially through the innovative "cap-and-trade" acid rain control program. The acid rain program has been a resounding success, cutting annual sulfur dioxide emissions in the first phase by 50 percent below allowed levels. Emissions were reduced faster than required, and at far less cost. Industry compliance has been nearly 100 percent, and the program only requires a handful of EPA [Environmental Protection Agency] employees to operate. This approach is vastly more effective, and cheaper—two-thirds cheaper—than the traditional "command-and-control" approach.

This program is clearly a model for success. President Bush wants to expand this program to include two new pollutants—nitrogen oxides and mercury—while also dramatically reducing the SO_2 emissions allowed by current law.

Building on the Clean Air Act

Reducing SO_2 and NO_x emissions will save hundreds of northeastern lakes and hundreds of thousands of acres of forests from acid rain. The President's Clear Skies Initiative is designed to help us meet our national air quality goals. A new Clean Air Act for the 21st century must build on this founding principle—modernization and better technology will mean a progressive new way to accomplish these long-standing environmental goals. The Clear Skies Initiative will continue to bring Americans:

- **Improved Air Quality**: Reducing air pollution will bring clean air to tens of millions of people, saving them from smog (ground-level ozone) and fine particulate matter (dust) that cause respiratory and cardiovascular distress.

- **Improved Health**: Reducing emissions of fine particulate matter will prolong thousands of lives and prevent thousands of new cases of chronic bronchitis, hospitalizations and emergency room visits. Reducing the formation of ground-level ozone, or smog, will bring healthier air to tens of millions of people, and reduce the number of ozone-related health problems such as respiratory infection, asthma attacks, and chronic lung damage. Reducing mercury emissions will reduce the risk of toxic effects from mercury exposure to children exposed during their mother's pregnancy.

- **Better Environmental Protection from Acid Rain, Smog, Haze, Mercury and Nitrogen Deposition**: Reducing SO_2 and NO_x emissions will save hundreds of northeastern lakes and hundreds of thousands of acres of forests from acid rain, particularly in the Adirondacks and other parts of the Appalachian Mountains. It will also improve visibility over much of the country, particularly the scenic vistas in national parks such as the Grand Canyon. Reducing emissions of nitrogen oxides will also reduce nitrogen deposition in water, improving coastal ecosystem health along the East and

Gulf coasts. Reducing mercury emissions will reduce mercury deposition in lakes and streams.

- **Secure, Affordable Power**: The Clear Skies Initiative will keep electricity costs low for consumers by saving as much as $1 billion each year in compliance costs. Power generators will have the flexibility to reduce emissions in the most cost-effective way. It will also encourage the continual improvement in technology to reduce emissions from coal-fired power plants in concert with the Department of Energy's Clean Coal Technology program and incentives for power plants that install "scrubbers" [technology that removes sulfur from coal exhaust] early in the program. Under the Clear Skies Initiative, America will continue to have a diverse fuel mix that ensures a reliable, affordable energy supply.

How the Clear Skies Initiative Works

To improve air quality for millions of Americans, the Clear Skies Initiative will adopt the lessons learned from 30 years of environmental regulation by:

Establishing Emission Reduction Targets, Based on Sound Science, That Will Significantly Improve Air Quality, Protecting Human and Environmental Health: By reducing air pollution, and conducting constant monitoring of emissions, the Clear Skies Initiative guarantees that America's power plants will meet ambitious air quality goals, even as they bring new power plants on line to meet growing demand. During the first phase, the EPA Administrator will review new scientific, technology and cost information and, if necessary, adjust the phase-two targets. This will include a vigorous research program to further understand the fate and transport of pollutants in the atmosphere.

Adopting a Comprehensive, Integrated, Multi-Pollutant Approach: By reducing emissions of the three key sources of air pollution at the same time, the Clear Skies Initiative will produce environmental results more effectively and efficiently than the current labyrinth of overlapping and uncoordinated single-pollutant requirements. The current approach is inefficient and ineffective, imposing unnecessarily high cost. . . .

Using the market-based mechanism of a cap-and-trade program, the Clear Skies Initiative will establish national, federally enforceable emissions limits.

Improving Environmental Performance at Lower Cost Using Market-Based Mechanisms That Create Incentives for Innovation: Using the market-based mechanism of a cap-and-trade program, the Clear Skies Initiative will establish national, federally enforceable emissions limits for each pollutant. Allowances are distributed to electricity generators, and the cap declines at specific intervals, 2010, and then again in 2018. Generators respond by gradually reducing their emissions— reducing more than the cap requires early in the program in order to save allowances for use later in the program when the caps decline. That is, generators respond to declining allowance caps just like people respond to declining income when they're planning for retirement: they do more now, investing and saving for the future. Individual generators can choose when to reduce their emissions in response to their particular circumstances and the price of allowances they see in the market. This encourages the least expensive reductions over time as well as across facilities.

Using the market-based mechanism of a cap-and-trade program, the Clear Skies Initiative will establish national, federally enforceable emissions limits.

At this point, the government only has to enforce the emission limits, distribute allowances and verify that each facility has sufficient allowances for their annual emissions. There's no need for lengthy, costly, uncertain litigation to enforce the law. Creative, innovative strategies to reduce emissions are immediately rewarded: facilities save money by finding innovative ways to reduce emissions more than a command-and-control law would require. This creates an incentive for continual improvement in environmental performance.

The flexibility in the process of allocating emission credits or allowances will also accommodate the different air quality needs in the East and the West while preserving fair competition. Western states have already made significant headway in identifying future SO_2 reductions necessary to meet air quality goals in the Western Regional Air Partnership ("WRAP") agreement between EPA, Western states, tribes, industry and environmental groups. SO_2 allocations will track this agreement. NO_x reduction caps for the East and West will also be set to accommodate these different needs, and separate East and West trading regions will be created.

Ensuring a Secure, Affordable Energy Supply: By setting firm caps while offering flexibility in how utilities can meet those caps, the Clear Skies Initiative preserves a diverse fuel mix that supports economic growth with reasonably priced energy. The firm caps and the adequate lead time create a predictable climate for long-term planning and capital investment in power generation, which will ensure an adequate energy supply. This will also create substantial cost savings to consumers.

The Cap and Trade System

The Clear Skies Initiative will deliver substantial health and environmental benefits through a market-based approach that rewards innovation, reduces costs, and ensures results. Instead of the government telling electricity generators precisely where and how to reduce their emissions—the old command-and-control approach—this market-based program tells them when and how much to reduce pollution by establishing a firm, maximum "cap" on emissions. The trading program creates incentives for electricity generators to reduce their emissions even more than the law requires, and more quickly than required. Electricity generators must hold an "allowance" for each ton of pollution they emit—one ton, one allowance. The government controls the number of allowances that are distributed and reduces them over time. Electricity generators must continually monitor and report their emissions.

Most importantly, these allowances can be traded freely. That means that if you're smart and creative, and you figure out a better way to reduce emissions, you get rewarded by making those reductions and selling unneeded allowances in the market. And, if you unexpectedly can't reduce emissions as much as planned, you have the flexibility to go out and buy more allowances in the market—all without any government interference, and without undermining air quality. This flexibility lets businesses figure out the cheapest way to reduce emissions while government sticks to setting the overall emission cap at a level that guarantees that industry meets ambitious air quality goals.

The cap ensures that the reductions in SO_2, NO_x and mercury required by the Clear Skies Initiative are achieved and maintained over time even as new power plants are built. The open trading program gives power plants the flexibility to choose how they meet their target emission reductions, which minimizes compliance costs and lowers consumer electricity prices.

Results of the Cap and Trade System

Cost Savings—The acid rain cap and trade program passed by Congress in 1990 achieved reductions at two-thirds the cost of achieving the same reductions under a command-and-control system. This program reduced more pollution in the last decade than all other Clean Air Act command-and-control programs combined during the same period.

Innovation—Trading under the acid rain program created financial incentives for electricity generators to look for new and low-cost ways to reduce emissions and to do so early.

Integrity—The acid rain cap and trade program has high accountability and transparency. Electricity generators must install monitors to prove that they have sufficient allowances to match their actual emissions.

Regional Effect—The acid rain program resulted in emission reductions well below the cap in the areas that contribute most of the sulfur in acid rain. Comparing emissions from the 263 power plants regulated in the first phase of the program in 1999 with those in 1990, the North Central, Southeast and Mid-Atlantic regions achieved 49 percent, 48 percent and 43 percent reductions in SO_2, respectively. Several analyses of trading under the acid rain program have concluded that the program did not result in local areas with higher emission levels ("hot spots").

Guaranteed Results—The Acid Rain program enjoys nearly 100 percent compliance and only takes 75 EPA employees to run—a track record no command-and-control program can meet. Reductions in the early years averaged 25 percent below the required cap. Emission cuts resulted in air quality improvements over a broad area of the U.S. and significant reductions in acid rain.

The Clear Skies Act Will Increase Pollution in Many Communities

John Walke

About the author: John Walke is the director of the Natural Resources Defense Council's clean air program.

Editor's note: The following viewpoint was presented as testimony before the U.S. Senate Committee on Environment and Public Works on February 2, 2005.

The [George W. Bush] Administration's [Clear Skies] bill[1] takes with one hand while it also takes with the other. In addition to allowing more pollution than public health can tolerate, the Administration's bill weakens or outright [re-]peals all of the specific programs and requirements in the current Clean Air Act that are effectively reducing power plant pollution today and that will reduce it further tomorrow.

The deletions, exemptions and weakening provisions in the Administration's bill do great damage to fundamental precepts of the Clean Air Act that have helped deliver cleaner air for over thirty years.

- Current law requires cleanup of polluted areas as quickly as practicable, but the Administration's bill grants automatic delays to 2015, and effective delays until 2023.

- Current law requires EPA [Environmental Protection Agency] to adopt rules to minimize toxic pollution from power plants, but the Administration's bill repeals

---

1. The bill failed to get enough votes to move to the full Senate in 2005. Another version of the bill was considered in the House of Representatives but as of October 2005 had not become law.

John Walke, "Dirty Skies: The 'Clear Skies Act of 2005' Would Harm the Public, Help Big Polluters and Worsen Global Warming," www.nrdc.org, February 2, 2005. Copyright © 2005 by the Natural Resources Defense Council, Inc. Reproduced by permission.

most of those requirements and replaces them with a weak performance requirement for mercury that is delayed ten years from the current law's schedule.

- Current law requires new sources locating in polluted areas to meet state-of-the-art pollution standards and avoid making existing health problems worse, but the Administration's bill exempts *all* sources (even those not covered by any cap) from those requirements until 2015, allowing more than a decade's worth of new pollution sources to make air quality worse.

- Current law gives states victimized by interstate pollution effective rights to remedy that pollution, but the Administration's bill makes those remedies ineffective against power plants and prohibits *any* reductions from power plants under these provisions until 2012.

- Current law requires new and modified power plants to limit pollution increases to avoid turning clean air areas into polluted areas, but the Administration's bill repeals this safeguard except for a narrow 30-mile circle around certain National Parks and wilderness areas.

- Current law requires new and modified power plants to meet up-to-date emission performance standards to protect areas with clean air, but the Administration's bill repeals this safeguard for nearly all existing plants and replaces it with a more polluting performance standard for new plants.

The Administration defends all of these dismantling provisions as eliminating programs that are not required since its plan establishes new national caps for certain power plant pollutants. But the current Administration ignores what the George H.W. Bush Administration recognized—that national caps cannot protect local air quality and must not override the tools that are in the law to protect communities from pollution increases that harm local air quality. Neither the Bush Administration nor Congress sought to repeal the tools that protect local air quality when enacting the acid rain cap program in 1990. Repeal of those tools is no more justified now. . . .

The Bill Does Not Meet Public Health Standards

The [Bush] Administration's bill postpones the attainment deadline for the country's unhealthy air areas by six years or more. As long as states could show that their polluted areas would attain the smog and soot standards by 2015, those areas would be labeled "transitional" rather than "nonattainment" and be granted automatic extensions of the deadlines to meet health standards. Since the requirement to attain the standards "as expeditiously as practicable" applies only to nonattainment areas, states would be under no obligation to bring air quality into line with the health-based standards any earlier than 2015.

The [Bush] Administration's bill postpones the attainment deadline for the country's unhealthy air areas by six years or more.

What is more, under the Administration's bill, there is no meaningful remedy for continued nonattainment. If an area is still violating an air quality standard in 2015, EPA makes a determination more than a year later (in 2017), and the responsible state submits a new state implementation plan up to three years after that—in 2020. The state then has at least until 2022 to achieve the air quality standard by implementing its plan. In other words, the Administration's bill forces as many as 159 million Americans to breathe harmful amounts of air pollution for six to eleven years longer than current law allows.

By labeling hundreds of polluted counties "transitional" rather than "nonattainment," the Administration's bill also allows *every* major industrial source built or modified in those areas to make health problems worse by evading the lowest achievable emissions rate ("LAER") and offset requirements of current law. Under current law, anyone wishing to build or modify a major source of air pollution in a "nonattainment" area must ensure that the source employs state-of-the-art methods to minimize its pollution (LAER) and must offset any added emissions so as not to degrade the already poor air quality in the area. This requirement applies not just to power plants, but to all other major air pollution sources (oil refineries, chemical plants, manufacturing facilities, etc.) as well.

Under the Administration's bill, these health safeguards no longer apply in areas relabeled "transitional." In other words, the Administration's bill makes it easier for the owners of oil refineries, chemical facilities, and power plants to churn out additional pollution in hundreds of counties where the air is already unhealthy to breathe. It is important to emphasize that while the Administration's bill caps only power plant emissions, the bill creates this loophole for *all* major industrial sources. Amazingly, the Administration has not offered a word of justification for this remarkable assault on the Act's public health safeguards.

The bill would also weaken the prevention of significant deterioration (PSD) program requirements that keep clean air areas from being degraded—by repealing the program as it relates to power plants and opt-in units. Instead of having to show protection of PSD increments (in the law since 1977), a new or modified plant would only have to show noninterference with the health standards. As a result, a new or modified power plant could increase emissions that degrade air quality all the way up to the level of the health standards.

The Bill Weakens Existing Safeguards Against Hazardous Air Pollution

The Administration's bill allows unrestricted emissions trading of mercury, something never before allowed under the Clean Air Act for any hazardous air pollutant. The current Clean Air Act requires mercury reductions at each power plant, based on the emissions reductions achievable through advanced technologies applied to individual emissions units. By allowing mercury trading, the bill allows some power plants not to reduce their emissions at all. Instead, they can buy mercury emission allowances from other power plants and do nothing to stop contamination of local lakes and streams. Some plants can even *increase* their mercury emissions.

By allowing mercury trading, the bill allows some power plants not to reduce their emissions at all. . . . Some plants can even increase their mercury emissions.

Indeed, EPA's own analyses of the Administration's bill acknowledge mercury pollution increases above today's levels from "specific sources in some states," due to the trading features of the bill and the bill's repeal of the 2008 MACT [maximum achievable control technology] standard. This dirtier outcome would not be allowed if the plant-specific MACT standard remained in effect. EPA's data also show that parts of New England, the Great Lakes, Gulf Coast region and other areas receive only very small reductions in mercury deposition under the bill.

What is more, the Administration's bill *exempts* from the mercury cap all coal-fired electric generating units that emit 50 pounds-per-year or less of mercury. Fifty-two percent of the nation's coal-fired electric generating units qualify for that exemption. *That is, the bill exempts 52 percent of the country's coal-fired units from the mercury cap.* These units emit 5.2 tons annually, which is equivalent to about one sixth of the total 2010–2017 mercury cap in the Administration's bill and one third of the 2018 cap. It is also approximately 10 percent of current power-plant mercury emissions in this country. The exemption applies even to units that are part of a multi-unit power plant that collectively emits more than 50 pounds-per-year of mercury. For example, the bill exempts all five of the units at a massive generating station in Wabash, Indiana, even though the plant collectively emits 134 pounds-per-year of mercury.

Reductions Are Fictional

Not only does the bill exempt 52 percent of all mercury-emitting power-plant units, it fails to require compensatory reductions from the 48 percent that remain in the trading program, thus hitting public health twice. That is, the touted 70 percent reductions are entirely fictional; 48 percent of plants must reduce their emissions 70 percent, while the remainder need not make any reductions at all. With respect to the polluters exempted from the mercury cap, the bill fails even to require that they monitor their mercury emissions.

Even for the units that are not exempt from the caps, the bill requires no mercury controls until 2010 (a two-year delay over the current law) and substitutes much weaker mercury caps in place of the plant-by-plant "maximum achievable control technology" ("MACT") requirement. For 2010 through 2017, the bill's 34-ton cap represents merely the mercury reductions incidental to the bill's phase-one caps for SO_2 and NO_x. Mercury cuts beyond these incidental reductions are not achieved until 2018. In other words, the Administration's 3-pollutant bill is effectively a 2-pollutant bill until 2018.

Also repealed with mercury MACT is the current law's requirement that EPA establish MACT standards for *all* hazardous air pollutants emitted by power plants, not just mercury. For hazardous pollutants other than mercury, the bill leaves only the authority to set "residual risk" standards through a complex risk-based process, but the earliest that those regulations are permitted to take effect is *2018*—a full 10 years after the MACT compliance deadline of the current Clean Air Act. Moreover, the bill repeals the Clean Air Act's "residual risk" protections *entirely* for mercury without regard to any health risks that remain under the bill's weaker mercury caps.

Because unrestricted trading of mercury emissions could lead to toxic hotspots where mercury contamination increases, the Clean Air Act—as well as other legislative proposals (notably the Clean Power and Clean Smokestacks Acts)—prohibit mercury trading. Hotspot-risks under the Administration's bill are made worse by the fact that the bill does not require continuous emissions monitoring systems ("CEMS") for mercury. EPA itself has identified continuous monitoring and reporting as design features essential to the environmental integrity of the acid rain trading program. Mercury emissions trading is allowed even without continuous monitoring so long as the Administrator determines that CEMS for mercury with "reasonable vendor guarantees" are not commercially available. The responsible approach would be to make any mercury trading (if some carefully limited program were shown to prevent hotspots) contingent on the development of reliable continuous monitoring systems for the pollutant.

Finally, with regard to all non-mercury air toxics, including human carcinogens, the Administration's bill exempts as many as 69,000 industrial units (boilers and process heaters, plywood and composite wood product manufacturing units, reciprocating internal combustion engines, and stationary combustion turbines) from the Clean Air Act's mandate of deep emissions reductions by 2008. The result is to override the removal of as many as 74,000 tons-per-year of toxic and even carcinogenic chemicals from the air we breathe. . . .

The Bill Eliminates Existing Safeguards Against Pollution Hotspots

Under the Administration's bill, a power plant can pollute at any level so long as it buys sufficient pollution allowances from other plants. The fact that power plant pollution may decline nationwide, however, provides no protection to the communities affected by a plant whose emissions stay level, or even increase, because of its owner's reliance on emissions trading. The "new source review" (NSR) provisions in the Clean Air Act provide important protection against the emergence of "pollution havens" or "hotspots" in response to an emissions trading system. NSR requires any person planning to build a new major pollution source, or to change an existing one in a way that will cause an emissions increase, to demonstrate that the source will use the most effective pollution control methods available and that its emissions increase will not degrade air quality locally, in downwind communities, or in National Parks.

Under the Administration's bill, a power plant can pollute at any level so long as it buys sufficient pollution allowances from other plants.

The Administration's bill eliminates federal new source review provisions for power plants and any non-power-plant facilities opting into the emissions trading scheme. If the bill is enacted, companies will be free to cause even massive pollution increases by building new plants or expanding old ones without adopting up-to-date pollution controls or determining whether air quality will worsen locally or downwind. . . .

The Bill Does Not Protect National Parks

The Administration's bill exempts owners of new and modified power plants from the obligation to meet up-to-date pollution performance standards and examine the impacts of any added pollution on National Parks or wildernesses—called "Class I areas"—(except those within 30 miles of the plant). The bill also eliminates the role of the federal land manager (typically the National Parks Service Superintendent for a National Park) in assuring that the air quality of these treasured lands is protected.

Under current law, if a new or expanded pollution source could affect a Class I area, the federal land manager has an opportunity to review the draft permit and an accompanying air quality analysis to assure that factors relevant to protecting national parks and wilderness areas are taken into consideration, and that harmful effects are mitigated. The federal land manager's review is eliminated under the Administration's bill for all plants farther than 30 miles from each park or wilderness.

The Administration's bill also repeals the current Clean Air Act program to lift the haze shrouding the Nation's parks by obligating the states to require the best available retrofit technology ("BART") on all major sources of air pollution built between 1962 and 1977 that contribute to the haze. The bill exempts all opt-in units and all power plants—the primary contributor to park haze—from the BART requirement. In so doing, the bill lets off the hook those intransigent companies that have not yet installed the best available retrofit technology on their plants.

If the Administration elected to enforce the requirement, instead of lifting it, the installation of BART on just the largest power plants would reduce annual SO_2 emissions by 4.5 million tons, and annual NO_x emissions by 1.9 million tons. Those reductions alone would be equivalent to what the

Administration's bill will purportedly achieve in its entire 8-10 year first phase.

In addition, EPA has before it a remand from the courts to issue a new rule to protect clean air in the Nation's parks; if EPA does its job properly, we can substantially reduce power plant pollution in the West as well as the East.

The Government Must Not Allow Drilling in the Arctic National Wildlife Refuge

Daniela Muhawi

About the author: Daniela Muhawi is a writer for EcoWorld, an Internet publishing company that provides information and resources on nature and clean technology.

If you are one of the few without a personal vehicle it is likely you take trips on the subway, bus, train or ferry. Ask almost anyone in the United States about their day and it will involve a car trip along one of the millions of crisscrossing streets that lace America like a giant spider web. Cars rush along the pavement filled with drivers on their way to pick up groceries, take the kids to school, go to work or to go on long road trips.

According to the American Petroleum Institute [API], there are "70 million more drivers on the road driving about 113 million more vehicles today than there were 30 years ago. Over this same period of time, drivers have increased the miles they each drive by about 44 percent, which means that vehicle miles traveled per year had increased by about 145 percent since 1970." The increased need for vehicles has come with an increased need for fuel.

Unfortunately, fuel isn't the most environmentally friendly energy source. Anyone who has walked behind a car and choked on the exhaust fumes knows it can't be good for the air.

Soon after the first cars left behind the noxious black smoke it became obvious that fuels needed some refining. It didn't take long for the gas industry to develop cleaner tech-

Daniela Muhawi, "Beyond the Brooks Range: What Is At Stake in Alaska Concerns More than Just Caribou," www.ecoworld.org, 2004. Copyright © 2004 by EcoWorld, Inc. All rights reserved. Reproduced by permission.

nology and fuels. Modern, unleaded fuels are less hazardous and less of a pollutant now. In fact, the U.S. EPA (Environmental Protection Agency) found that vehicle emissions have declined 41% since 1970 despite the increased amount of vehicles on the road. However, that does not mean that all problems associated with fuel have been solved. Far from it.

Technology Alters the Environment

A major issue is the process of retrieving crude oil from the earth. Pipe leaks, accidents during transport and spills are still commonplace. The American Petroleum Institute claims that many steps are taken to "assure that oil and natural gas can be produced with minimal environmental impact." API also provides some examples: "Directional drilling technology allows us to access oil and gas resources that underlie a sensitive area, such as a wetland, from an area nearby where a drilling rig can safely be located. In the Arctic, companies build ice roads and ice drilling pads that melt away in the spring. . . . Companies have substantially reduced the amount of land disturbance required for drilling a well and by drilling several wells from a single location (with directional or multi-lateral technology) require a much smaller number of sites to achieve the same level of production."

These spills don't only affect the drilling site but lands adjacent as well.

Yet even with impressive technological advancements in the drilling industry, oil rigs and human intrusions still alter the environment and often devastate habitats. Brian Moore, legislative director of the Alaska Wilderness League, knows just how harmful drilling can be. "Prudhoe Bay has 400 toxic spills a year," he says with concern. "That's more than one spill a day. These spills don't only affect the drilling site but lands adjacent as well. Devastating effects are real and clear. Environmentalists have not made them up." It is hard to forget the oil covered seabirds, otters and seals that slowly died after 10 million gallons of crude oil spilled from the *Exxon Valdez* in 1989. Naturally, environmentalists cringe when plans arise to drill in an area full of wildlife. The possibility that drilling may take place in Alaska's Arctic National Wildlife Refuge (ANWR), an area renowned for unique wildlife and pristine habitat, is a shock to any nature lover.[1]

The Refuge constitutes the last 5% of the Alaskan North Slope not open to drilling. . . . The Refuge is the last area wildlife can live peacefully.

The Last Refuge

Drilling in the Alaskan Wildlife Refuge will definitely leave its mark. Moore explains that drilling in the refuge will have devastating effects: "Oil exploration is planned to take place in the most critical and sensitive area of the refuge. 130,000 caribou, the last large migrating mammal in the U.S. migrate hundreds of miles to calf here in late May and June, in this one area, and this is where they want to put oil rigs! Gravel roads and drained wetlands are not conducive to them giving birth. It is also devastating to denning polar bears. The polar bear population is already declining and is already threatened by extinction. Oil drilling and extraction may increase the odds of losing the species. Native Alaskans, Gwich'in Indians whose life revolves around this piece of land will have the most important thing in their culture, the calving ground, taken away from them. [Gwich'in Indians, rely on the migratory Porcupine Caribou herd as a key source of food and clothing.] It is cultural genocide." To make matters worse, the Refuge constitutes the last 5% of the Alaskan North Slope not open to oil drilling. Drilling operations already exist through-

---

1. On March 16, 2005, the U.S. Senate passed the vote (51-49) to allow drilling in ANWR.

Polar bears are one of the many species environmentalists fear will suffer as a result of oil drilling in the Arctic National Wildlife Refuge in Alaska. © Lowell Georgia/CORBIS

out the rest of the area. The Refuge is the last area wildlife can live peacefully.

The oil industry argues that they will only leave a small footprint in the Arctic, covering a mere 2000 acres—the size of the Dallas Airport. Yet these measurements do not realistically represent the areas affected by these drilling operations. Vinay Jain, a spokesperson for the National Wildlife Federation, is skeptical of the oil industry's skewed measurements. "They have said it will only cover 2000 acres," he says, "but the problem lies in the fact that they are condensing. If you realistically measure the areas influenced by oil rigs, it is really spread out. Think of it as a spider web: When the web is spread out, it covers a very large area but when you ball it up it is only a fraction of its original size. They [the oil industry] are giving you the number made up of all the rigs without counting the area in between—the industry is giving you the balled up number. Roads and platforms, these things are all spread out and cause fragmentation of habitat. It isn't just one solid area of 2000 acres, it's much more."

Sneaky Strategies

The Republican Party has had an obvious interest in the Arctic refuge's oil wells. As the former owner of Arbusto Energy Inc. and Bush Exploration, American President [George W.] Bush has always had an interest in oil. Vice President [Dick] Cheney, also a former oil man, had experience being the CEO of the world's largest oil service company—the Halliburton Company. It is not surprising then, that oil companies have connections with the government. Defenders of Wildlife note that oil and gas firms have donated $1,761,567 to Bush's presidential campaign, making them one of the highest contributors and therefore also the most influential. Exxon Mobil Corp., Conoco Phillips and BP PLC are some of the companies enthusiastic about drilling in the Arctic National Wildlife Refuge.

Recent Republican gains in the Senate could give President Bush a real chance of opening the Alaska wildlife refuge to drilling. For one thing, four Republican senators who favor drilling in the refuge were elected [in] early November [2004] and replaced Democrats who opposed the proposal in 2003. These new members could make all the difference when voting to drill in the Arctic. There is also a sneaky strategy involved to guarantee success for pro-drilling groups: By attaching drilling to the federal budget resolution it becomes a filibuster-proof strategy. The budget resolution would instruct the House Resources Committee to generate savings over the next few years. This goal would be accomplished by identifying new revenue sources, one of which would be the revenue created by selling oil leases in the Arctic refuge.

Jain is disappointed with the strategy: "It [attaching drilling revenues to the budget] is a fairly undemocratic way of doing things. This is a way of avoiding an honest and open debate. It is not the right way to decide an issue as important as this. A fair and open debate is the proper way to handle this situation and the drilling proposals should be distinct from the budget bill, which was never intended for this purpose."

So why is drilling in the Arctic so important? Moore is surprised with the oil industry's interest there as well: "Why are they so interested in drilling in the Arctic refuge? It's hard to understand. It's not about the oil. The House Majority Leader, Tom DeLay (R-Texas), gave a speech [in 2003] admitting that it's all about the precedent. He essentially said that if we can drill in the Arctic Refuge we can drill anywhere. Opening the Arctic to oil exploration will open other lands for future use by the oil Industry." According to Moore, "It starts with the Arctic Wildlife Refuge, and then it'll be Yellowstone, the Grand Canyon or the coast of California. It's not about the oil. The Coastal Plain [of Alaska] is the last bit of Arctic coast left. The oil industry would want nothing more than to put a fence of oil rigs around Alaska. Its crazy to me, but it seems that that's what they want. Like a bunch of drunken sailors; they are on a binge and the only thing they want is more oil and more land to suck it out of."

The oil industry would want nothing more than to put a fence of oil rigs around Alaska.

Jain explains that "the amount of oil in the refuge is marginal at best. It is not going to make a difference. Drilling in the Arctic Refuge is symbolic of a larger effort. It's about getting into one protected area and using the momentum to get into another."

Drilling Will Not Reduce Dependence on Foreign Oil

The Bush administration officials claim that drilling in the Arctic will enhance U.S security by reducing dependence on imported oil. They also promote this controversial venture by stating that drilling will reduce the country's energy shortages.

However, very little electrical power comes from oil. Another argument states that drilling will reduce the oil prices. The American Petroleum Institute explains how this would work: "Crude oil prices are established in world markets responding to supply and demand. New discoveries are crucially important to supply. Every barrel of oil produced domestically is one less barrel that must be purchased from foreign sources. In the long term, additional U.S. supplies help to hold down crude oil prices because demand for crude oil from non-U.S. sources is lower than it would be without added domestic production. . ."

Moore explains that "the argument they put forth is that drilling will reduce our dependency on foreign oil. The Department of Energy, however, stated that if we started drilling today, oil would not reach peak production till after 2020 and if oil is in fact present, it would only reduce oil dependency by about 2%." It is assumed that the oil present in Alaska is not enough to meet even a fraction of America's needs. Projections in 1998 showed a 95% chance of finding three billion barrels of oil and a 5% chance of finding 10.5 barrels of oil. 3 billion barrels of oil would barely supply enough oil to last half a year in the U.S. It is hard to believe that drilling in Alaska will benefit U.S citizens since any oil that exists will take about a decade to reach the market and estimates on the amount of oil in the area are speculative. Further more, prices will not fluctuate from drilling in Alaska since the amount of oil found in the refuge is minimal.

Reduce Demand for Oil

Eventually though, there will be no where else to drill when we have exhausted all other resources. Jain believes the best solution is to look for additional energy resources and reduce demand for oil before it gets to that point. "Reducing demand for oil is a better strategy then drilling a pristine corner of Alaska to increase supply, especially when there's relatively little oil there. When we think about ways to meet America's energy needs we tend to turn towards oil, however we can still maintain an American lifestyle with alternative energy. The technology is out there. Hydrogen is something that may be promising years down the road, but in the short term, we can save a lot of oil by making cars more fuel efficient. By simply increasing the average fuel economy by a few gallons we would save much more oil than we would get from drilling in the refuge. The new Honda Accord Hybrid is more powerful than the regular Accord. The idea that you have to give up one thing [power] to be environmentally sound is a false one. You can have a fuel efficient car that is also more powerful. . . . We can't just drill our way to energy independence."

Alaska's Arctic National Wildlife Refuge was founded over 40 years ago by President [Dwight D.] Eisenhower. He wanted to preserve this pristine area. It is a sad fact that Congress wants to abandon 44 years of legacy. This wildlife refuge is one of the last pristine areas on earth. Caribou, grizzlies, polar bears, wolves, thousands of birds and countless other animals make this unique area their home. This pristine habitat should not be turned into an industrial zone.

The battle for this area is symbolic and it is important for conservationists and the American public in general to realize this. "This is one of the last pristine areas in America," Jain says. "We know we are not going to reduce gas prices and reduce independence on foreign oil by drilling here. If we can't conserve this tiny sliver of habitat for future generations what does that say about our priorities?"

The Government Should Allow Drilling in the Arctic National Wildlife Refuge

John K. Carlisle

About the author: John K. Carlisle is the director of the Environmental Policy Task Force for the National Center for Public Policy Research, a conservative communications and research foundation.

The environmental movement's vehement objection to President George W. Bush's vow to open Alaska's Arctic National Wildlife Refuge (ANWR)[1] to oil exploration is showing Americans suffering from high energy prices that the environmental movement is no friend of theirs.

Environmentalist contentions that oil drilling in the vast refuge poses an unacceptable risk to wildlife and the pristine forests is unfounded, given, among other things, that oil drilling equipment would cover a mere .1 percent of ANWR's 19 million acres.

But what is most worrisome for environmentalists about the ANWR clash is that the debate comes at the worst possible time for them, a time when the priority of recession-worried consumers is maximizing energy affordability, not indulging environmentalists' excessive hostility to fossil fuels.

American Consumers Hit by Multiple Energy Price Hikes

American consumers are being hit hard by energy price increases in many ways, several of which are directly attributable to environmental policies:

1. On March 16, 2005, the Senate voted to allow drilling in ANWR.

John K. Carlisle, "Environmentalists' Opposition to Oil Exploration in the Arctic National Wildlife Refuge is Unfounded," *National Policy Analysis*, January 2001. Copyright © 2001 by the National Center for Policy Analysis. All rights reserved. Reproduced by permission.

The price of gasoline has soared more than 60 percent from 90 cents per gallon in April 1999 to $1.45 per gallon today [January 2001]. This increase has largely been driven by planned production cutbacks by the Organization of Petroleum Exporting Countries (OPEC) which have sent the cost of a barrel of oil skyrocketing to $35 per barrel from less than $10 per barrel in December 1998. Imported oil now accounts for 57 percent of U.S. oil needs, so any OPEC policy change is sure to significantly affect the American economy. It is also unlikely that OPEC is going to provide relief to beleaguered consumers in the near future. The Energy Information Administration (EIA) estimates that OPEC crude oil production will continue to decline [in 2001] from a production rate of 26.5 million barrels to 26.1 million barrels per day. Oil prices are likely to hover around $30 per barrel for 2001, higher than $28.75 in 2000 and significantly higher than 1999's average of $17.50.

OPEC is only part of the problem. The federal government is exacerbating oil price inflation by making it increasingly difficult for the energy industry to access vast amounts of natural gas and oil located within the U.S. Sixty-seven percent of the nation's onshore oil reserves and 40 percent of natural gas reserves are located on federal land in the western U.S. But environmentalists have been very successful in gradually removing much of this land from new energy development. Since 1983, the amount of federal land available for development has decreased by more than 60 percent.

The latest environmental salvo against domestic energy development occurred on January 5, 2001, when President [Bill] Clinton announced a ban on new road construction on 58 million acres of federal land. While some environmentalists called it the "greatest conservation achievement in history," the roadless rule marks yet another dramatic assault on the hard-pressed energy industry's ability to find new fuel sources.

Lack of Refineries Hurts Consumers

Environmental regulations that make it nearly impossible to build new oil refineries are further compounding the nation's energy woes. No major refineries have been built in the U.S. since the mid-1970s, even though the number of vehicles in use has doubled. This lack of refinery capacity especially hurts Californian and Midwestern consumers. Last summer [in 2000], Californians were paying $1.85 per gallon and Midwesterners as much as $1.87 per gallon, considerably more than the 2000 summer national average of $1.68 per gallon. A lack of refineries during this peak travel season was the reason.

Environmental regulations that make it nearly impossible to build new oil refineries are further compounding the nation's energy woes.

Overall, the nation's crude oil stocks are now seven percent below the five-year average with little prospect in sight for a quick increase in U.S. petroleum production.

A raft of onerous Environmental Protection Agency (EPA) regulations that unnecessarily inflate the price of gasoline is yet another cause of U.S. energy woes. A U.S. House Science Committee report concluded that Midwestern consumers were forced to pay 50 cents more per gallon in the summer of 2000 due to the EPA's controversial requirement that one-third of the nation's gasoline supply must be reformulated gasoline (RFG), a requirement imposed to promote cleaner air. The EPA ordered the costly RFG regulation despite a 1999 report from the National Research Council concluding that the RFG regulation would not reduce air pollution. . . .

Natural gas is not immune to this across-the-board energy inflation. The cost of natural gas has tripled over the past two years, rising from $2 per thousand cubic feet in January 1999 to $6 per thousand cubic feet in January 2001. The EIA believes that natural gas prices will remain high throughout the heating season due to minimal storage levels.

Natural gas is of special concern because it is the primary energy source required to fulfill the nation's huge need for electricity. Although 15 percent of U.S. electrical generating capacity is fired by natural gas, 95 percent of the new proposed generating capacity is gas-fired. The long-term outlook for gas prices is not good because most large reserves of natural gas are located in ANWR and the western U.S., areas that the federal government has increasingly closed off to energy development.

The coming debate over ANWR between the Bush Administration and the environmental movement will be crucial. ANWR is the nation's single largest oil reserve. Some petroleum experts say that ANWR has at least 9.2 billion barrels of oil while others say it may contain as much as 16 billion barrels. ANWR's natural gas resources are equally impressive: an estimated 34 trillion cubic feet of gas. U.S. Senator Frank Murkowski of Alaska, Chairman of the Senate Energy and Natural Resources Committee, says ANWR is so oil-rich it could substitute for the oil the U.S. would otherwise have to import from Saudi Arabia over the next 30 years. Opening ANWR could reduce oil imports by about eight percent.

Environmental Objections to Opening ANWR Are Unfounded

Environmentalists argue that opening ANWR will turn millions of acres of scenic land into a bleak landscape of ugly derricks, leaking pipelines, oil spills, and dying wildlife.

There is no truth to this shrill warning.

Drilling would only take place within the 1.5 million-acre coastal plain. Congress has set aside 17.5 million acres of ANWR as wildlife areas where no exploration will be allowed, an area about the size of the state of South Carolina. ANWR is only a small percentage of the publicly-protected land in Alaska. There are currently 322 million acres of publicly-owned land in Alaska.

ANWR is the nation's single largest oil reserve.

When President Clinton vetoed 1995 legislation that would have opened ANWR to drilling, he claimed that the "pristine" and scenic coastal plain is the biological heart of the refuge and would be ruined by energy development.

This is false. To begin with, this supposedly pristine area is already home to a village of Inupiat Native Americans, complete with an airstrip, power lines and an oil well. (Incidentally, the Inupiats strongly support ANWR oil development.) The coastal plain also contains a military early warning radar site. Second, the coastal plain is not the most scenic part of ANWR. Environmentalists often show pictures of the Brooks Range and other scenic parts of ANWR to convey the impression that the coastal plain is similarly scenic. But the coastal plain is a flat, treeless, nearly featureless plain that extends from the ocean to the Brooks Range. The Brooks Range is scenic hills and mountains that would not be affected by drilling. Temperatures frequently plunge to 40 degrees below zero in winter, making it uninhabitable for most animals.

Wildlife Is Not Harmed by Oil Production

Most of the refuge's abundant wildlife is located in the non-coastal plain and would be safe from oil development projects. Strict federal laws already require companies to protect the environment during oil and gas operations on federal land. For example, the Marine Mammals Protection Act protects the polar bears in Alaska's extensive oil fields on the North Slope 60 miles to the west of ANWR. There has been major oil drilling in the North Slope area for more than two decades without endangering species or causing other ecological disasters. At the North Slope's Prudhoe Bay, which produces 1.4 million barrels per day and accounts for 25 percent of domestic oil production, workers must follow numerous strict rules regarding wildlife. For instance, there are steel cages around many of the doors at production facilities so workers can make sure there are no polar bears present before venturing outdoors. Thanks to the commitment to protect wildlife, not a single polar bear has been killed or injured due to oil operations at Prudhoe Bay.

Most of the refuge's abundant wildlife . . . would be safe from oil development projects.

Although environmentalists claim that oil exploration at ANWR poses an ominous threat to wildlife, there is not one species of animal from either the North Slope or the ANWR coastal plain that is listed as endangered.

Other environmental rules on North Slope drilling, which would also be in place for ANWR drilling, include seasonal restrictions on construction, temporary roads protecting the ecologically important permafrost, and elevated pipelines permitting the passage of caribou and other wildlife. The Central Arctic caribou herd near Prudhoe Bay has grown from about 3,000 in 1970 to 23,000 by 1995. In some respects, the North Slope environment has improved after more than 20 years of drilling.

There is no reason to doubt that ANWR's caribou would be safe from drilling. When the caribou migrate to ANWR from Canada during the spring thaw in late May or early June, the herds pass at least 89 dry Canadian wells and cross a highway. There is no evidence that these structures hinder the animals' migration practices. Oil drilling would only occur during the winter months because of the need for ice airstrips, ice roads and ice platforms. There is no caribou present during these winter months.

Some environmentalists argue that it is vital to protect the ANWR coastal plain because it is the last five percent of the Arctic coastline that is not being drilled. This is not true. Only 14 percent of the 1,100 mile Arctic coastline is open to oil exploration.

A Small Amount of ANWR Land Would Be Required

A major misconception, encouraged by environmentalists, is that opening the ANWR coastal plain to oil exploration would cover a large part of the 1.5 million acre plain with drill rigs and other production.

Nothing could be further from the truth.

The lesson of Prudhoe Bay is again informative. Drilling rigs, production facilities and gravel roads cover only 5,000 acres of the 250,000-acre Prudhoe Bay field. Hence, oil companies can recover 1.4 million barrels of oil per day from Prudhoe Bay using a mere two percent of the land area.

But the news gets even better for ANWR. Because of advances in oil drilling technology, the petroleum industry can recover oil using even less land than was required for Prudhoe Bay, which was developed using 1960s-era technology. In the 1970s, production wells were spaced 100 feet or more apart. But thanks to new directional drilling techniques and drilling equipment, wells can now be placed 25, 15 or in some cases even just 10 feet apart. An oil field that would have covered 65 acres in 1977 will cover less than nine acres today [in January 2001]. If Prudhoe Bay had been developed using this new technology, oil equipment and roads would cover 1,526 acres, a reduction in land area of more than 60 percent.

Recovery of the potentially larger reserves of oil located in ANWR would require covering as little as 2,000 acres of the ANWR coastal plain's 1.5 million acres. Reducing the land area needed for exploration is not the only ecologically beneficent action being taken by the oil industry. Instead of constructing gravel pads for exploration drilling, companies can build pads out of ice. Thus when a dry exploration well is capped, the ice pad will melt and leave little evidence of human activity. Likewise, temporary ice roads can extensively be used to support winter exploration activities, as is currently done on the North Slope.

Developing ANWR Will Not Harm the Environment

Contrary to what many environmentalists believe, developing ANWR and the nation's energy industry will not harm the environment. The facts clearly show that Alaska's Prudhoe Bay is being aggressively developed and making a major contribution to domestic oil production without harming wildlife or scarring the landscape. Due to advances in technology, ANWR's coastal plain can also be opened to oil exploration with an even greater certitude that species will be protected, with even less impact on a small percentage of the coastal plain's landscape and the preservation of ANWR's considerable scenic beauty.

Contrary to what many environmentalists believe, developing ANWR . . . will not harm the environment.

Environmental objections to opening ANWR are simply unfounded. By opposing development of ANWR without legitimate ecological grievances, the environmental movement is unnecessarily condemning the American consumer to even higher gasoline prices and utility bills. When President Bush makes the case to Congress this year [in 2001] for opening ANWR, the environmental movement is poised to set itself in opposition to the American people, whose chief economic grievance will likely be high energy costs. This will not be an enviable position for environmental groups, especially given that a poll conducted [in 2000] by the *Christian Science Moni-*

tor found that Americans support opening ANWR to oil exploration by a solid margin of 54 to 38 percent. During the debate, environmentalists are going to have to explain to Americans everywhere, from Northeasterners suffering from skyrocketing heating oil bills to Californians experiencing fourfold increases in electric bills, why they should continue to sacrifice their standard of living on the altar of the environmental movement's irrational inflexibility.

Whatever explanation environmentalists will offer, it is unlikely to satisfy these besieged energy consumers.

The Endangered Species Act Should Be Strengthened

Jamie Rappaport Clark

About the author: Jamie Rappaport Clark is the executive vice president of Defenders of Wildlife, an organization dedicated to the preservation of wildlife and native plants.

Editor's note: This viewpoint is excerpted from Jamie Rappaport Clark's testimony before the House Resources Committee Hearing on H.R. 3824, "Threatened and Endangered Species Recovery Act of 2005," on September 21, 2005.

Prior to coming to Defenders of Wildlife, I worked for the federal government for almost 20 years, for both the Department of Defense and the Department of the Interior. I served as Director of the U.S. Fish and Wildlife Service from 1997 to 2001. Thus, I have seen the Endangered Species Act [ESA] from different perspectives: that of an agency working to comply with the law; leading the agency charged, along with other federal agencies, states, and private landowners, with implementing the law; and now leading a conservation organization working to ensure that the law is fully implemented to conserve threatened and endangered plants and wildlife.

The common lesson I have drawn from all of these experiences is that the Endangered Species Act is one of our most farsighted and important conservation laws. For more than 30 years, the Endangered Species Act has sounded the alarm and saved wildlife that we humans have driven toward extinction. Today [2005], we have wolves in Yellowstone, manatees in Florida, and sea otters in California, largely because of the Act. We can still see bald eagles in the lower 48 states and other magnificent creatures like the peregrine falcon, the

Jamie Rappaport Clark, testimony before the U.S. House Committee on Resources, Washington, DC, September 21, 2005.-

American alligator, and California condors, largely because of the Act.

Success of the Endangered Species Act

With the Endangered Species Act's help, hundreds of species have been rescued from the catastrophic permanence of extinction. Indeed, there can be no denying that, with the Endangered Species Act's help, hundreds of species have been rescued from the catastrophic permanence of extinction. Many have seen their populations stabilized; some have actually seen their populations grow. Some have even benefited from comprehensive recovery and habitat conservation efforts to the point where they no longer need the protections of the Act.

In so many ways, Congress was prescient in the original construction of the Endangered Species Act. First, it crafted an Act that spoke specifically to the value—tangible and intangible—of conserving species for future generations, a key point sometimes lost in today's discussions.

With the Endangered Species Act's help, hundreds of species have been rescued from the catastrophic permanence of extinction.

Second, it addressed a problem that, at the time, was only just beginning to be understood: our looming extinction crisis. Currently there is little doubt left in the minds of professional biologists that Earth is faced with a mounting loss of species that threatens to rival the great mass extinctions of the geological record. Human activities have brought the Earth to the brink of this crisis. Many biologists today say that coming decades will see the loss of large numbers of species. These extinctions will alter not only biological diversity but also the evolutionary processes by which diversity is generated and maintained. Extinction is now proceeding one thousand times faster than the planet's historic rate.

Lastly, in passing the Act, Congress recognized another key fact that subsequent scientific understanding has only confirmed: the best way to protect species is to conserve their habitat. Today, loss of habitat is widely considered by scientists to be the primary cause of species endangerment and extinction.

Reduced to its core, the Act simply says the federal government must identify species threatened with extinction, identify habitat they need to survive, and help protect both accordingly. And it has worked. More than 1800 species currently protected by the Act are still with us; only 9 have been declared extinct. That's an astonishing success rate of more than 99 percent. It highlights that the first step toward recovering a species is to halt its decline.

More than 1800 species currently protected by the Act are still with us; only 9 have been declared extinct. That's an astonishing success rate of more than 99 percent.

With this record in mind, the benchmark against which to measure any proposal to change the Act is: Does it truly aid species conservation? If the answer is no, then we have failed.

Reform of the Act Undermines Species Recovery

Mr. Chairman [Rep. Richard Pombo], you have been quite critical of the Act for not doing a better job of recovering species. The Act can be improved to better promote species recovery. Unfortunately, the bill you have introduced [to reform the Endangered Species Act], H.R. 3824, is very disappointing. Instead of promoting recovery, H.R. 3824 would deal a tremendous setback to the recovery of threatened and endangered species.

H.R. 3824 undermines species recovery in several ways:

1. H.R. 3824 Fails to Protect Habitat H.R. 3824 establishes new recovery planning requirements that fail to ensure that habitat necessary for species recovery will be adequately protected or even considered in determining, under section 7 of the Act, whether agency actions are likely to jeopardize the continued existence of threatened and endangered species. Thus, the bill's elimination of critical habitat without providing an improved way of protecting habitat essential to species recovery is a significant step backward, one that seriously undermines the purpose and intent of the law.

2. H.R. 3824 Weakens Obligation to Consult H.R. 3824 significantly weakens the substantive and procedural protections of section 7, generally considered the Act's most important and effective provision. For example, authorizing the Secretary [of the Interior] to establish undefined "alternative procedures" for complying with section 7 could all but eliminate the current requirement that each federal agency consult with the Services on "any action" which is likely to harm endangered or threatened species. Further, H.R. 3824 creates several exemptions from the requirements of section 7 with respect to section 10 conservation plans and section 6 cooperative agreements. If federal agencies are not even required to engage in section 7 consultation, the bill makes it highly unlikely that they will do anything to promote species recovery.

3. H.R. 3824 Exempts from Prohibited Take of Endangered Species Landowners will be able to secure de facto exemptions from the Act simply by waiting 91 days. H.R. 3824 creates a broad and unwarranted de facto exemption from the current prohibition against take of an endangered species, contained in section 9 of the Act. Under H.R. 3824, a landowner can demand from the Secretary a written determination of whether a proposed activity will violate the take prohibition. If the Secretary fails to respond within 90 days, the bill provides that this shall be deemed a determination that the activity will not result in a take. Given the overburdened U.S. Fish and Wildlife Service, bogged down already in a morass of missed deadlines, it is easy to see how landowners will be able to secure de facto exemptions from the Act simply by waiting 91 days. Not only will this impede species recovery, it may result in piecemeal whittling away of important habitat, thereby accelerating species extinctions.

4. H.R. 3824 Weakens Protection of Threatened Species H.R. 3824 undercuts prospects for recovery of threatened species as well as endangered species. Currently, section 4 of the Act requires regulations for threatened species that meet a highly protective standard: "necessary and advisable for the conservation" of the species. In other words, under current law, the Secretary is required to issue regulations that are necessary and advisable for the recovery of threatened species. H.R. 3824 eliminates any requirement whatsoever for regulations protecting threatened species. Moreover, even where the Secretary chooses to issue a regulation for a threatened species, H.R. 3824 eliminates the protective standard for such regulations.

5. H.R. 3824 Weakens Scientific Foundation for Endangered Species Decisions The bill virtually guarantees continued problems implementing the Act, further reducing the likelihood of species recovery. H.R. 3824 weakens the role of science in virtually every decision under the Act. Language requiring scientific information to comply with the Data Quality Act, to be empirical, peer-reviewed, and consistent with yet-to-be-written regulations before it can be considered the "best scientific data available" creates new procedural hurdles that threaten to exclude important scientific information such as population modeling and projections. Moreover, by failing to provide additional resources to comply with these new requirements, while maintaining and adding new deadlines, the bill virtually guarantees continued problems implementing the Act, further reducing the likelihood of species recovery.

6. H.R. 3824 Eliminates Act's Ultimate Safety Valve H.R. 3824 eliminates the Cabinet-level Endangered Species Committee, established by Congress in 1978 to resolve truly irreconcilable conflicts between species conservation and development. The exemption provisions contained in section 7(e)–(n) have only rarely been used, testifying to the Act's flexibility for resolving conflicts. Nevertheless, the availability of the Endangered Species Committee, with its power to decide the ultimate fate of a species, has served as an important caution sign and an essential safety valve for conflict resolution. Eliminating it will only lead to further controversy over species conservation, rather than promoting species recovery.

7. H.R. 3824 Requires Paying Corporations Not to Violate the Law H.R. 3824 requires taxpayers to pay developers, corporations, and others the fair market value of any use of their property which is determined to violate the prohibition against take of an endangered species. Under the bill, developers are not required to first avail themselves of the Act's permit procedures under section 10 or, if a federal permit is involved, section 7 consultation. There is no requirement that the proposed activity be more than speculative and there is no limit on the number of times a developer can receive compensation for different proposed activities on his or her land. Thus, a developer might propose construction of a shopping center that will wipe out the habitat of an endangered species. Once the developer has been compensated for that use, he or she can propose an office park on the site and become entitled to compensation again. Instead of promoting species recovery, this provision creates a windfall for developers and corporations, requiring taxpayers to pay them over and over again for not killing or injuring endangered species.

Improving Species Recovery Under the Act

Mr. Chairman, your bill, H.R. 3824, will not make the Endangered Species Act do a better job at recovering species or improve the Act generally. Those goals are achievable, however, if this Committee and the Congress will take a more productive path. The following steps would improve the Act and ensure it works better for all stakeholders: . . .

1. Make species recovery the central focus of the Act The goal of the Act is to conserve species and the ecosystems upon which they depend. Section 3(3) of the Act defines conservation as "the use of all methods and procedures which are necessary to bring any endangered species or threatened species to the point at which the measures provided pursuant to this Act are no longer necessary." In other words, the goal of the Act is to recover species. Implementing that goal has, however, been elusive.

We can make the ESA more effective for species and less onerous for landowners by ensuring that federal agencies do their part to promote species recovery. That means making sure that federal agencies are held to a high standard. If federal agencies are allowed to do things that make recovery less likely to occur, that push recovery off into the distant future, or that increase the cost of recovery, not only will species conservation suffer but the regulation of private landowners and others will almost certainly increase. Yet, federal agencies have been allowed to do exactly that.

Section 7 of the Act requires all federal agencies to consult with the Secretary of the Interior or Commerce to insure that their actions are not likely to jeopardize the continued existence of a listed species or adversely modify or destroy critical habitat. However, there is no statutory definition of jeopardy in current law. The only definition of jeopardy is regulatory and several courts have now found that definition invalid because it ignores the effects of an action on species recovery.

As federal agencies have ignored the effects of their actions on recovery of species, recovery has become an ever more distant goal. Consequently, the burden on private landowners to make up for what the federal agencies have not done has grown ever greater. If you really want to make the Act more effective at recovering species and less burdensome for private landowners, you can do that in one simple step: define jeopardy in the Act so that agencies insure that their actions will not make it less likely that a species will recover or significantly delay or increase the cost of recovery.

The goal of recovering species and, therefore, the defini-tion of jeopardy, should be clear and unambiguous, without any qualifications such as "in the long-term." The addition of that phrase creates a serious risk that actions that have sub-stantial adverse impacts on a species, but are of short dura-tion, may not be seen as jeopardizing the continued existence of the species. By adopting an unambiguous definition of jeopardy, Congress will make clear that the central goal of the Act is to recover species and that section 7 consultations on federal agency actions must assess whether the actions are likely to impair recovery.

We can make the ESA more effective for species and less onerous for landowners by ensuring that federal agencies do their part to promote species recovery.

---

2. Properly protect and manage habitat that is needed for spe-cies recovery Since species recovery is the central goal of the Act, the key step in achieving that goal is properly protecting and managing habitat necessary for species recovery. Since species recovery is the central goal of the Act, the key step in achieving that goal is properly protecting and managing habi-tat necessary for species recovery. Accordingly, the Act should make clear that the habitat necessary for recovery needs to be identified and protected. The recovery plan is the logical and appropriate place to achieve this.

Section 4(f) of the Act requires the Secretary to develop and implement recovery plans. In order to make these plans truly effective in achieving species recovery, several changes should be made. First, there should be a deadline for develop-ing recovery plans, perhaps 36 months from the date a species is listed. Second, specific areas of land or water that are of particular value to the conservation of the species and that are likely to require management or protection in order to ac-complish the goals of the recovery plan should be identified. Third, there should be a clear requirement that, in considering whether a federal agency action is likely to jeopardize a listed species, the effects of the action on the habitat identified in the recovery plan must be considered.

Adoption of these measures, in combination with a clear statutory definition of jeopardy tied to a recovery standard, could eliminate the need for designation of critical habitat. If such measures were adopted, designated critical habitat should be treated as habitat necessary for recovery in the interim while habitat necessary for recovery is identified.

3. Enhance the science underlying species conservation There has been much debate over the quality of science underlying endangered species conservation decisions. Unfortunately, most of the proposals to address this, including H.R. 3824, have focused on restricting the types of data that can be considered or requiring time-consuming and cumbersome peer-review of virtually all conservation decisions. Rather than throwing more roadblocks in the way of consideration of the best available science, as the Act requires, you should increase the scientific capacity of the FWS [U.S. Fish and Wildlife Service] and NMFS [National Marine Fisheries Service] by creating for each of them a science advisory board modeled after the very successful science advisory board of the EPA [Environmental Protection Agency]. In that manner, rather than having Congress tell these agencies how they should do science—Congress can give them the benefit of useful input from scientifically qualified authorities.

4. Promote greater partnerships with the states An important way to strengthen the Act is to take full advantage of the experience, expertise, and other strengths of state fish and wildlife and conservation agencies. The role of the states in the conservation of imperiled species should be strengthened and improved by fostering a stronger partnership between the states and the federal government. Currently, section 6 of the Act calls generally for cooperation between state and federal governments, but specifically addresses only the acquisition and management of land. Section 6 should be amended to specify that there be consultation with the State agencies concerned regarding revisions of the list of endangered species and threatened species, development and implementation of recovery plans, acquisition of lands, waters, or interests therein, issuance of permits, and measures to direct attention and resources to species before they become endangered or threatened.

An important way to strengthen the Act is to take full advantage of the experience, expertise, and other strengths of state fish and wildlife and conservation agencies.

As a further step in this direction, section 6 should be amended to replace the current system of "full authorities" and "limited authorities" cooperative agreements, with a simpler and more meaningful approach. States should have the flexibility to enter into cooperative agreements covering as many—or as few—species as the states choose. For each species covered by a proposed agreement, the state must demonstrate that it has an "adequate and active conservation program" that includes scientific resource management of such species and that is consistent with the purposes and policies of the Endangered Species Act. The allocation of federal funds to the states in support of their programs should be based on a somewhat shorter, but more meaningful set of criteria. First among these is the number of species to which the cooperative agreement applies. In addition, strong enforcement provisions, species recovery requirements, and adequate funding and staffing to implement state endangered species programs should be considered.

5. Provide incentives for conservation on private lands Most private landowners are good stewards of their land. The Act should encourage this conduct by providing financial and regulatory incentives for conservation. Using existing programs, such as the Partners for Fish and Wildlife program and Farm Bill conservation programs to contribute to the conservation of endangered species should be encouraged. Providing landowners with safe-harbor assurances for their voluntary actions promoting species conservation should likewise be encouraged. Establishing a program to provide financial assistance for the implementation of conservation measures under safe-harbor agreements would also encourage the broader use of such agreements.

6. Significantly increase funding for the Act Everyone knows the U.S. Fish and Wildlife Service and NOAA [National Oceanic and Atmospheric Administration] are chronically underfunded to carry out their responsibilities under the Endangered Species Act. Interestingly, it would not take much to change that. Devoting a mere fraction of the money the government spends on roads, mines, timber hauls and other "habitat-busting" projects instead to endangered species conservation would pay dramatic dividends, both for species conservation and for the regulated community waiting for decisions on permits and plans.

Increased Effectiveness

When Congress adopted the Endangered Species Act more than thirty years ago, it made a commitment to future generations to protect and restore endangered species and their habitat. As this Committee considers changes to the Act, you should ask yourselves whether you are keeping that commitment. H.R. 3824 reneges on that commitment by undermining the Endangered Species Act's effectiveness at recovering threatened and endangered species. The changes I have outlined today would make the Act more effective in conserving species and, in so doing, keep the Endangered Species Act's commitment to our children, grandchildren, and generations to come.

The Endangered Species Act Should Be Abolished

William F. Jasper

About the author: William F. Jasper is a lead investigator and senior editor for the New American, *a conservative magazine that provides news analysis.*

During a recent forest fire, help for trapped firefighters was delayed out of fear that it might harm the "endangered" bull trout. Result: The fish were saved; four firefighters died.

A crew battling a wildfire makes a radio request for a helicopter water drop. Fighting forest fires is always hot, exhausting, dangerous work, and in the tinderboxes which are our grossly mismanaged national forests, a momentary delay can be deadly. If you're the radio dispatcher who receives the request, what do you do?

A) Immediately order the water drop.

B) Deny the request because the drop may risk harming an "endangered" fish.

C) Relay the request to "higher authorities" who will dither for hours trying to determine whether departmental policy allows suspension of the fish rules in order to help the firefighters.

For any normal, rational person, the decision is a no-brainer. But today, when the supposed interests of "endangered" dung beetles, snail darters, suckers, and gnatcatchers regularly trump those of mere humans, federal employees are not allowed the luxury of normalcy and rationality.

On July 10th [2001], four firefighters battling a blaze in Washington state's Okanogan National Forest were killed by

William F. Jasper, "Saving Fish Before Firefighters," *The New American*, vol. 17, September 10, 2001. Copyright © 2001 by American Opinion Publishing, Inc. Reproduced by permission.

the fire, after waiting more than nine hours for a requested water drop. Trapped by flames, Tom Craven, 30, Devin Weaver, 21, Jessica Johnson, 19, and Karen Fitzpatrick, 18, tried to survive by huddling in their fire-resistant survival tents. The tents merely served as their death shrouds. A co-worker, Jason Emhoff, survived but was severely burned.

When the supposed interests of 'endangered' dung beetles ... regularly trump those of mere humans, federal employees are not allowed the luxury of normalcy and rationality.

The tragic death toll was very nearly much, much higher. Seventeen additional fire crew members and two hikers narrowly escaped the fatal blaze.

Bureaucratic Bumbling

Early on the morning of July 10th, an elite team of firefighters known as "Hot Shots" had contained what came to be known as the "Thirty Mile Fire." At 5:30 a.m. they requested a helicopter water drop to help douse the fire. They were informed that one would not be available until 10 a.m. Expecting the arrival of the chopper, the Hot Shots turned over the fire to a "mop-up" crew.[1] In the drought-dried, brush-choked national forests of the western states, the fire hazard increases dramatically as morning temperatures begin to rise and the dew evaporates. Winds can quickly whip a "contained" fire into an inferno.

The mop-up crew waited for the promised water drop. It didn't come at 10 o'clock. By noon it had still not arrived, so the crew made another request. "At 12:06, the dispatch office ordered the helicopter," Jan Flatten, the environmental officer

---

1. A portion of the regular crew assigned to removing burning material near control lines after a fire has been contained or controlled.

for the Okanogan and Wenatchee National Forests, told FOX News on August 1st [2001]. "However, because there were endangered species in the Chewuch River, they wanted to get permission from the district in order to dip into the river."

The great fear was that the bucket used by the helicopter to scoop up water might accidentally also scoop up an endangered bull trout. According to Flatten, the dispatch office couldn't reach anyone with the authority to approve the helicopter drop. Forest Service District Commander John Newcom, Fire Manager Peter Sodoquist, and a biologist huddled for two hours to determine whether or not they could grant an exemption for the helicopter drop.

"That time lag of about two hours was when they were trying to locate someone with the authority to tell them they could go ahead and take water out of the Chewuch River," said Flatten. Still unexplained is why it took the officials from 5:30 a.m.—when the request was first made—until noon to attempt to convene their high privy council.

Eventually, permission was given for the helicopter mission. Around 3 p.m., more than nine hours after the initial request, the helicopter drop finally came. By then it was too late; the fire was rapidly spreading. In short order, it grew from 25 acres to 2,500 acres, trapping the firefighters.

The fire crew made a desperate attempt to flee in their vans. Pete Kampen, a seven-year firefighter and the fire's crew-boss trainee, got seven firefighters into a van and down the road, racing a wall of flames that threatened to cut off any escape route. "We just flat gunned it. It's the first time I've been really scared," an Associated Press story quoted Kampen as saying. The remaining 14 crew members were following in a second van but the towering inferno blocked their path and drove them back. They were forced to abandon their vehicle and take refuge in their fire tents. Two hikers trapped by the soaring flames stumbled onto the crew and one of the young firefighters gave them refuge in her shelter, even though it is designed for single occupancy. Ten of the stranded crew members and the two hikers survived the harrowing ordeal; four did not.

Deadly Endangered Species Act

At a July 31st [2001] hearing of the Forests Subcommittee of the House Resources Committee, Rep. Scott McInnis (R-Colo.) stated: "I am very, very concerned. We need to find out if there was a delay putting water on this . . . because of the Endangered Species Act [ESA]."

The bureaucrats ran for cover. The U.S. Fish and Wildlife Service issued a press release on August 1st denying "allegations" that there had been any delay in water delivery to the fire due to the ESA. "The U.S. Fish and Wildlife Service wishes to clarify that wildland fires represent an emergency under the Endangered Species Act and that in no circumstances is emergency response to be delayed or obstructed because of Endangered Species Act considerations," declared the agency.

Federal employees in the field know that rules protecting 'endangered' species are sacrosanct, and any violation may cost them their job.

If that is *official* policy, it obviously is not the *de facto* operating policy guiding people in the field. In practice, federal employees in the field know that rules protecting "endangered" species are sacrosanct, and any violation may cost them their job. They have seen the "rights" of spiders, spotted newts, and plovers trump human rights many times. They have seen timber towns and loggers shut down for spotted owls and farmers arrested for accidentally killing rats while plowing their fields. They've seen farmers have their water cut off in the middle of a drought for the supposed benefit of sucker fish. They have seen federal SWAT teams descend on an elderly rancher for shooting a wolf that was killing his livestock.

Federal bureaucrats may have paper directives hidden in their desks for the purpose of absolving them of the consequences of their draconian policies, but the reality is that the institutional mind-set is one in which designated "endangered" species must be protected *at all costs*. The Endangered Species Act has been wreaking havoc for decades and the Thirty Mile Fire is not the first time the ESA has taken human lives.

The ESA Should Be Abolished

In 1992, environmental extremists used the ESA to stop controlled burns of dangerous brush build-ups, claiming the preventive actions would endanger protected gnatcatchers and rats. Fire authorities warned that deadly infernos awaited unless the brush was burned early in the year. The environmentalists, with their attorneys and media support, won. But nature had its way. Propelled by strong "Santa Ana" winds and fueled by the protected brush, wildfires consumed more than 150,000 acres, inflicting more than half a billion dollars in damage. More than 500 homes were lost or damaged in the disaster. Some 30,000 people were forced to evacuate their properties. Three people lost their lives. Thousands were left temporarily homeless. And many endangered gnatcatchers were killed by the flames and most of their habitat was destroyed.

Millions of acres of federal forests are now clogged with unnatural fuel buildup, thanks to "endangered species" regulations that have set the fuse on more tragedies to come. These tinderboxes are awaiting only a spark to burst into raging, deadly forest fires that will certainly take more human lives, while destroying resources, habitat, and many of the very species the ESA ostensibly was crafted to protect. The ESA has repeatedly proven itself completely impractical in accomplishing its stated objectives. But this unconstitutional act has been very effective at destroying the rights of American citizens and transferring enormous power to the federal bureaucracy. The Endangered Species Act should not be reformed; it should be abolished.

CHAPTER 4

How Can Society Conserve the Environment?

Chapter Preface

In the first half of 2005 almost one hundred thousand hybrid automobiles were sold to consumers across the United States—a 255 percent increase from the same period in 2004. Today, consumers are willing to wait four months or more to purchase a Toyota Prius, Honda Civic Hybrid, Ford Escape Hybrid, or the many other hybrids recently hitting the market. As America's dependence on foreign oil increases and global warming scares seem to be in the news daily, many Americans are turning to hybrid vehicles as one way to help conserve the environment.

Hybrids use battery-powered electric motors to assist a gasoline engine. When a driver needs to suddenly increase speed to make a lane change, or traverse a steep hill, or even idle in rush hour traffic, the electric motor takes over. However, when the car is moving at a consistent speed, which means it's at its most efficient state, the gasoline engine switches on. Since the car relies on computers to more carefully control the flow of gasoline, and more efficient catalytic converters to power the engine, gasoline is saved and emissions are reduced. The twenty-one toxic pollutants from vehicle emissions are some of the biggest contributors to air pollution. The fuel-efficient hybrid technology greatly reduces the amount of pollutants that are released into the air from tailpipes and leaky exhaust systems. For instance, according to the California Air Resources Board, the 2003 Toyota Prius was 90 percent cleaner than the average model car in 2003. Christa Wagner of the Sierra Club states, "Hybrid cars are a proactive, practical way to improve air quality because they have reduced tailpipe emissions and they also save money at the pump."

While hybrids have many proponents, critics note that the high cost of the vehicles negates the dollars saved from using less gas. Since the average hybrid costs $3500–6000 more than a comparable standard car, it might take fifteen years before the gasoline savings make up the difference of the cost of the vehicle. However, the typical car owner keeps a vehicle for only six years on average. Joe White, the Detroit bureau chief of the *Wall Street Journal*, briefly considered purchasing a Toyota Prius until he investigated the cost of the vehicle. He states, "At least in my case the math didn't work out. I'd be behind when I got done financing a Prius, which costs more than a typical compact car of the same size, despite the fact that the Prius has much better mileage. The bottom line is, oddly enough, that gas isn't expensive enough to justify the switch to a hybrid for a lot of people."

Another criticism of hybrid vehicles is the lower than advertised expected fuel efficiency. Many hybrid owners have been discouraged that the gas mileage their hybrids get does not match the 40 or 50 miles per gallon advertised. Part of the problem is that the Environmental Protection Agency has not updated its system for measuring fuel efficiency in nineteen years, so it does not accurately measure the fuel efficiency of hybrid cars. Until the test for measuring fuel efficiency is updated, some critics feel that consumers will be misled by false advertisements. According to Pete Blackshaw, a disappointed Honda Civic Hybrid owner, "Nothing is more viral than a false advertising claim. That's why it is so important that manufacturers set clear expectations."

As with many efforts to protect the environment, the purchasing of hybrid cars has its detractors and supporters. The debate over how society can best conserve the environment is likely to continue well into the future.

Using Renewable Energy Will Help Conserve the Environment

Lester R. Brown

About the author: Lester R. Brown is an environmentalist and the president and founder of the Earth Policy Institute, an organization dedicated to achieving an environmentally sustainable economy. He has written extensively on global environmental issues, including Plan B: Rescuing a Planet Under Stress and a Civilization in Trouble.

As world population has doubled and the global economy has expanded sevenfold over the last half-century, our claims on the environment have become excessive. We are asking more of the Earth than it can give on an ongoing basis and creating a "bubble" economy—one in which economic output is artificially inflated by over-consumption of the Earth's natural resources.

We are cutting trees faster than they can regenerate, over-grazing rangelands and converting them into deserts, over-pumping aquifers and draining rivers dry. On our cropland, erosion exceeds new soil formation, slowly depriving the soil of its inherent fertility. We are taking fish from the ocean faster than they can reproduce. We are depleting our nonrenewable fossil fuels and releasing carbon dioxide (CO_2) faster than nature can absorb it, creating a greenhouse effect. As atmospheric CO_2 levels rise, so does the Earth's temperature.

The resulting mega-threat—climate change—is not getting the attention it deserves, particularly from the United States, the nation responsible for one fourth of all carbon emissions. Washington wants to wait until all the evidence on climate

Lester R. Brown, "Turning on: Renewable Energy," *Mother Earth News*, April/May 2004, p. 100. Copyright © 2004 by Ogden Publications, Inc. All rights reserved. Reproduced by permission.

change is in, by which time it will be too late to prevent a wholesale warming of the planet. As the Earth's temperature rises, it affects all life on the planet. Climate change will cause intense heat waves, more destructive storms, lower crop yields, glacier melting, and rising seas.

It Is Possible to Reduce Global Warming

To head off disaster, we must design more efficient transportation systems; raise efficiency standards for buildings, appliances and automobiles; and develop and promote renewable energy technology.

To head off disaster, we must design more efficient transportation systems; raise efficiency standards for buildings, appliances and automobiles; and develop and promote renewable energy technology.

The good news is that although this is a staggering challenge, it is entirely doable, and many countries are now taking action. Detailed studies by governments and environmental groups reveal the potential for reducing carbon emissions while saving money in the process. Cutting global carbon emissions in half by 2015 is entirely within range. Ambitious though this seems, it is commensurate with the threat climate change poses.

A lack of leadership, not a lack of technology, is why the United States' goal for cutting carbon emissions contrasts with Germany's. National and local governments, corporations and environmental groups are coming up with ambitious plans to cut carbon emissions. Prominent among these is a plan by British Prime Minister Tony Blair to reduce carbon emissions 60 percent in the United Kingdom by 2050. Blair and Sweden's Prime Minister, Goran Persson, are jointly urging the European Union to adopt the 60-percent goal, the amount scientists deem necessary to stabilize global atmospheric (CO_2) levels. . . .

In April 2003, the World Wildlife Fund released a peer-reviewed analysis that proposed reducing carbon emissions from U.S. electric-power generation 60 percent by 2020. This proposal focuses on more energy-efficient power-generation equipment; more efficient household appliances, industrial motors and other equipment; and a shift from coal to natural gas. If implemented, it could result in national savings averaging $20 billion a year until 2020.

The accelerating rise in the Earth's temperature calls for simultaneously raising efficiency standards and shifting to renewables in order to cut carbon emissions in half. The initial large gains are likely to come with efficiency improvements from mandating efficiency standards for household appliances, automobiles, and the construction of new buildings.

Setting New Standards

Of course, each nation will have to fashion its own plan for raising energy productivity. Nevertheless, a number of potential common components exist. These include banning nonrefillable beverage containers, eliminating incandescent light bulbs, doubling the fuel efficiency of automobiles, and redesigning urban transport systems.

Canada's Prince Edward Island has banned the use of non-refillable beverage containers, and Finland's stiff tax on non-refillables has led to 98-percent container reuse for soft drinks. These actions reduce energy use, water use and garbage generation. A refillable glass bottle used over and over again requires 90 percent less energy per use than an aluminum can, even if the can is recycled. Banning inefficient non-refillables is a win-win policy because it will cut both energy use and garbage flow.

Another simple step is to replace incandescent light bulbs with compact fluorescent bulbs (CFLs), which only use one-third the electricity and last 10 times longer. In the United States, 20 percent of electricity is used for lighting. If each household replaces incandescents with CFLs, electricity needed for lighting could be cut in half. CFLs yield a risk-free return of 25 percent to 40 percent a year. Their cost is falling, and they typically pay for themselves in electricity savings in a few years. Worldwide, replacing incandescent light bulbs with CFLs could save enough electricity to close hundreds of coal fired power plants, and it could be accomplished within three years, if we decided to do it.

Most automobile-centered systems are highly inefficient because most cars carry only the driver.

A third way to raise energy efficiency is to produce more efficient automobiles. In the United States, if all motorists shifted to cars with hybrid engines, such as the Toyota Prius or the Honda Insight, gasoline use could be cut in half. Sales of hybrid cars, introduced into the U.S. market in 1999, reached an estimated 46,000 in 2003, and the Prius was named "2004 Car of the Year" by *Motor Trend* magazine. Higher gasoline prices and a tax deduction for purchasing these vehicles are boosting sales and making the cars more cost-competitive; with U.S. auto manufacturers coming onto the market, hybrid-vehicle sales are projected to reach 1 million by 2007.

Cutting carbon emissions also means restructuring our transportation systems. Most automobile-centered systems are highly inefficient because most cars carry only the driver. Constructing well-developed light-rail systems, hydrogen-fueled buses as needed, and bicycle- and pedestrian-friendly lanes could increase mobility, reduce air pollution, and provide exercise. These improvements are much needed in a world where 3 million people die each year from urban air pollution, and where half or more of the adults in exercise-deprived, affluent societies are overweight. Fewer automobiles also means some parking lots could be converted into parks.

Harnessing the Wind

Wind energy offers a powerful alternative to fossil fuels—it is abundant, inexhaustible, widely distributed and clean, which is why it has been the world's fastest growing energy source over the last decade. Wind energy doesn't produce sulfur dioxide or nitrous oxides that cause acid rain, and it does not disrupt the Earth's climate. It also doesn't generate health-threatening mercury or pollute streams like coal-fired power plants.

Harnessing the wind also is cheap: Advances in wind-turbine design have reduced the cost of wind power to less than 4 cents per kilowatt-hour at prime wind sites—well below the price of nuclear power or coal. On prime sites, wind power can now even compete with gas, currently the cheapest source of electricity generation.

Even more exciting, with each doubling of world wind-generating capacity, costs fall by 15 percent. The recent growth rate of 31 percent a year means costs are dropping by 15 percent about every 30 months.

While natural-gas prices are highly volatile, the cost of wind power is declining. And, there is no OPEC (Organization of the Petroleum Exporting Countries) for wind.

By the end of 2002, world wind-generating capacity had increased sixfold to 31,100 megawatts—enough to meet the residential needs of Norway, Sweden, Finland, Denmark, and Belgium combined.

Germany, with more than 12,000 megawatts of wind power at the end of 2002, leads the world in generating capacity. Spain and the United States, at 4,800 and 4,700 megawatts, are second and third, respectively. Tiny Denmark is fourth with 2,900 megawatts, and India is fifth with 1,700 megawatts. A second wave of major players is coming onto the field, includ-

This wind farm in California generates power which is then sold to power companies.
© Lester Lefkowitz/Reuters/CORBIS

ing the United Kingdom, France, Italy, Brazil, and China. Europe has enough easily accessible offshore wind energy to meet all of its electricity needs, and China can easily double its current electricity generation from wind alone.

Enormous Potential for Wind

Globally, ambitious efforts to develop wind power are beginning to take shape. Germany is proposing a 30-percent cut in greenhouse-gas emissions throughout Europe by 2020—developing the continent's wind-energy resources is at the heart of this carbon reduction effort. And the United States is following Europe's lead. A 3,000-megawatt wind farm in South Dakota, designed to partly power the industrial Midwest surrounding Chicago, is one of the largest energy projects of any kind. Cape Wind is planning a 420-megawatt wind farm off the coast of Cape Cod, Massachusetts, and a newly formed energy company, called Winergy, has plans for some 9,000 megawatts in a network of wind farms stretching along the Atlantic coast.

In the United States, a national wind resource inventory published in 1991 indicates enough harnessable wind energy exists in just three states—North Dakota, Kansas and Texas—to satisfy national electricity needs. Today, this greatly understates U.S. potential: Recent advances in wind turbine design and size have dramatically expanded the wind-power industry.

It is time to consider an all-out effort to develop wind resources, given the enormous wind-generating potential and the associated benefits of climate stabilization. Instead of doubling wind-power generation every 30 months or so, perhaps we should aim to double wind-electric generation each year for the next several years. Costs would drop precipitously, giving wind-generated electricity an even greater advantage over fossil fuels.

It is time to consider an all-out effort to develop wind resources, given the enormous wind-generating potential and the associated benefits of climate stabilization.

Cheap electricity from wind is likely to become the principal source for electrolyzing water to produce hydrogen. Hydrogen can be transported through pipelines to power residential and industrial buildings; it also can be stored in power plants and used when the wind ebbs. The hydrogen storage and distribution system—most likely an adaptation of existing natural-gas systems—provides a way of both storing and transporting wind energy.

The incentives for switching to a wind/hydrogen system could come partly from restructuring global energy subsidies—shifting the $210 billion in annual fossil fuel subsidies to the development of wind energy, hydrogen generators, and kits to convert engines from gasoline to hydrogen. The investment capital could come from private capital markets and from companies already in the energy business: Energy giants Shell and BP have begun investing in wind power, and major corporations such as General Electric and ABB, a company that produces technology systems, are now in the wind-power business.

Solar Energy Rises

In recent years, a vast new market for solar power has opened in developing nations that are not yet linked to an electrical grid. About 1.7 billion people in developing nations do not have electricity, but as the cost of solar cells declines, it often is cheaper to provide electricity from solar cells than from a centralized source.

In [South American] Andean villages, solar-power systems are replacing candles. For villagers paying installation costs over 30 months, the monthly payment is roughly the same as the cost of a month's supply of candles. Once the solar cells are paid for, the villagers essentially have a free source of power that can supply electricity for decades.

At the end of 2002, more than 1 million homes in villages in the developing world were getting their electricity from solar cells. But this is less than 1 percent of the estimated 1.7 billion people who do not have electricity. The principal obstacle slowing the spread of solar-cell installations is not the cost, but the lack of small-scale credit programs to finance them. As this credit shortfall is overcome, purchases of solar cells could climb far above the rate of recent years.

The principal obstacle slowing the spread of solar-cell installations is not the cost, but the lack of small-scale credit programs to finance them.

The residential use of solar cells also is expanding in industrial countries. In Japan, where companies have commercialized a solar roofing material, some 70,000 homes now have solar installations. Consumers in Germany receive low-interest loans and a favorable guaranteed price when feeding excess electricity into the grid. In industrial nations, most installations reduce the consumer's dependence on grid-supplied electricity, much of it originating from coal....

Building the Hydrogen Economy

The evolution of the fuel cell—a device that uses an electro-chemical process to convert hydrogen into electricity—is setting the stage for the evolution of a hydrogen-based economy. The fuel cell is twice as efficient as the internal combustion engine and emits only water vapor. The fuel cell facilitates the shift to a single fuel—hydrogen—that neither pollutes nor disrupts the Earth's climate. Stationary fuel cells can be installed in the basements of buildings to heat, cool, and generate electricity for lights and appliances. Mobile fuel cells can power cars and portable electronic devices, such as cell phones and laptop computers. Hydrogen can come from many sources, including water, natural gas, or gasoline.

Iceland already has a plan to convert from fossil fuels to hydrogen. In 2003, the government, working with a consortium of companies led by Shell and DaimlerChrysler, took the first step by beginning to convert the capital city of Reykjavik's fleet of 80 buses from internal combustion to fuel cell engines. Shell built a hydrogen station to service the buses, using inexpensive hydroelectricity to produce clean hydrogen. In the next stage, Iceland's automobiles will be converted to fuel cell engines. And in the final stage, the Icelandic fishing fleet—the centerpiece of its economy—also will convert to fuel cells. Iceland already heats most of its homes and buildings with geothermal energy and gets most of its electricity from hydropower and geothermal power, and by 2050, plans to be the first modern economy to declare independence from fossil fuels.

On Yakushima Island, an 875-square-kilometer island off the southern tip of Japan, retired corporate executive Masatsugu Taniguchi is creating a hydrogen economy. The island receives more than 300 inches of rainfall a year, so Taniguchi plans to build small dams to convert the abundant hydropower into electricity to power hydrogen generators. The first goal will be to meet the needs of the island's 14,000 residents. Then, Taniguchi plans to ship hydrogen to main-land Japan. He says the island can export enough to run 500,000 automobiles.

More than 50 fueling stations equipped with hydrogen technology have opened around the world. In the Munich, Germany, airport, a hydrogen station fuels 15 airport buses with hydrogen-burning internal combustion engines. The United States now has more than a dozen hydrogen stations, mostly in California, although they are open only for demonstrations and research, not for public use.

Hydrogen is the fuel of choice for the new fuel cell engines every major automobile manufacturer is developing. In 2002, the Honda FCX and the Toyota FCHV-4 became the first fuel-cell-powered automobiles to appear on the market. Daimler-Chrysler also manufactures a fuel cell car called the F-cell, and Ford is following close behind. The evolution of fuel cells and advances in wind-turbine design create the hope that U.S. farmers and ranchers, who own most of the country's wind rights, could one day supply much of the electricity and fuel for cars in the United States.

Merging Wind Power and Hydrogen

In the end, the central question with hydrogen is whether it is made using renewable energy to electrolyze water, or with climate-disrupting fossil fuels. Natural gas likely will be the main source of hydrogen in the near future, but, given its abundance, wind has the potential to become the principal source in the new energy economy. The hydrogen storage and distribution system provides ways of storing and transporting wind energy efficiently—it is a natural marriage. Thus, countries that are rich in wind and rather sparsely populated, such as Canada, Argentina and Russia, could export hydrogen. Eastern Siberia, for example, could supply vast amounts of hydrogen to China, South Korea, and Japan.

In the United States, energy consultant Harry Braun made a proposal at an April 2003 Renewable Hydrogen Roundtable to quickly shift to a wind/hydrogen economy. He noted that if wind turbines were mass-produced like automobiles, the cost of wind-generated electricity would drop to 1 or 2 cents per kilowatt-hour.

Rather than wait for fuel cell engines, Braun suggests using hydrogen in internal combustion engines of the sort developed by German auto manufacturer BMW. He calculates that the production of hydrogen and high-efficiency, hydrogen-fueled engines would bring the cost of hydrogen down to $1.40 per equivalent-gallon of gasoline. If we make this conversion a priority, it can happen in two to three years. . . .

The hydrogen storage and distribution system provides ways of storing and transporting wind energy efficiently—it is a natural marriage.

If we decided for climate-stabilization reasons that we wanted to double wind-electric generation each year, wind could become the dominant source of electricity. The United States, for example, now has nearly 5,000 megawatts of wind-generating capacity. Doubling that each year would take it to 640,000 megawatts in seven years and make it the leading source of electricity. And this is not beyond the capacity of the industry: In 2001, wind-electric generating capacity grew by 67 percent. The total investment needed to reach this level of generation, using the rule of thumb of $1 million per megawatt (which is now on the high side), would be $640 billion over a seven-year span, or roughly $90 billion a year. For perspective, Americans currently spend $190 billion a year on gasoline.

While subsidies are being shifted from fossil fuels to renewables and the hydrogen economy infrastructure, it would make eminent sense to reduce income taxes and raise taxes on climate-disrupting energy sources at the same time. This tax shifting, already under way in several nations in Europe, helps consumers of energy—both individuals and corporations—understand the full costs of burning fossil fuels.

Although shifting subsidies and taxes are at the heart of the energy transformation that is needed, other policy tools can either increase efficiency or accelerate the shift to renewables and the hydrogen based economy. For instance, national and local governments, corporations, universities and individual homeowners can buy green power. In the United States, even if green power is not offered locally, a national Green Power Partnership electricity market operated by the Environmental Protection Agency enables anyone to buy green power. As more users sign up, the incentive for energy companies to produce green power increases.

As wind energy expands, the next step would be to close coal-fired power plants or use them to back up wind. Coal-fired plants are the most climate disruptive energy source because coal is almost pure carbon. Coal burning also is the principal source of the mercury deposits that contaminate freshwater lakes and streams. The prevalence of mercury-contaminated fish has led 44 state governments in the United States to issue warnings to consumers to limit or avoid eating fish from their locales. In 2001, the Centers for Disease Control and Prevention warned that 375,000 babies born each year in the United States are at risk of impaired mental development because of mercury exposure.

Although some industry groups and governmental bodies complain that reducing carbon emissions is costly and a burden on the economy, study after study concludes it is possible to reduce carbon emissions while making money in the process. The experience of individual companies confirms this. DuPont, one of the world's largest chemical manufacturers, already has cut its green-house-gas emissions from its 1990 level by 65 percent. In an annual report, CEO Charles Holliday Jr. proudly reports savings of $1.5 billion in energy-efficiency gains from 1990 to 2002.

It has become clear that incorporating renewable energy is one of the most profitable investments many companies can make, and as the true costs of climate change—withering crops, rising sea levels, and wildlife extinction—become apparent, companies that ignore the need to phase out fossil fuels will ultimately disappear. The companies that prosper will be the ones that adapt to a modern economy fueled by clean, renewable energy.

Renewable Energy Is Too Costly

James M. Taylor

James M. Taylor is managing editor of Environment & Climate News.

A pair of British studies released in March and April 2004 show relying on wind power or other non-nuclear "renewables" to reduce air pollution or carbon dioxide emissions forces consumers to pay at least twice as much as they currently pay for electricity generated from fossil fuels or emissions-free nuclear power.

Royal Academy

On March 10 [2004], the Royal Academy of Engineering released a study, "The Cost of Generating Electricity," comparing the costs of generating electricity from a number of energy sources. "The objective of this study," stated the Academy, "is to provide decision makers with simple, soundly based indicators of the cost performance for alternative electricity generation techniques. In order to make sensible decisions about energy policy, policy makers need to be able to compare the costs and benefits of different types of electricity generating technologies on a like for like basis."

According to the study, "The relationship between the cost of generating electrical power from various sources and the price that consumers pay is blurred by direct and indirect subsidies, market mechanisms, transmission, and distribution costs. The true costs of generating electrical power are often obscured by commercial sensitivities and competing claims

James M. Taylor, "British Studies Show Prohibitive Cost of Renewable Energy," www-.heartland.org, June 1, 2004. Copyright 2004 © by The Heartland Institute. Reproduced by permission.

that make the determination of sensible energy policy difficult and often imprecise."

Fossil fuels were found by the [Royal] Academy [of Engineering] to be half as expensive as renewable energy sources.

After cutting through the hidden taxpayer subsidies and market constraints that frequently mask the true costs of electrical power generation, the Academy concluded, "Our cheapest electricity will come from gas turbines and nuclear stations, costing just 2.3 p/kWh (British pence per kilowatt hour), compared with 3.7 p/kWh for onshore wind and 5.5 p/kWh for offshore wind farms."

"This may sound surprising, especially as we have included the cost of decommissioning in our assessment of the nuclear generation costs," said Academy Vice President Philip Ruffles, who served as chairperson for the study. "But modern nuclear stations are far simpler and more streamlined than the old generation and far cheaper to build and run."

Even fossil fuels were found by the Academy to be half as expensive as renewable energy sources—even after the Academy assigned a penalty to fossil fuel sources to take into account the costs of mitigating carbon dioxide emissions to a level required by the Kyoto Protocol, which Britain has pledged to support.

Fossil fuels were found by the [Royal] Academy [of Engineering] to be half as expensive as renewable energy sources.

Hume Institute Touts Nuclear Power

A study titled "Tilting at Windmills," released April 18 [2004] by Scottish economist David Simpson of the David Hume Institute, bolstered the Royal Academy's findings. According to Simpson, generating electricity through wind power and other non-nuclear renewables costs twice as much as generating power.

Generating electricity through wind power and other non-nuclear renewables costs twice as much as generating power from conventional sources.

Achieving the British government's goal of 20 percent of generation of energy through non-nuclear renewable sources, concluded Simpson, will cost British citizens well more than a billion dollars per year. Additionally, according to the study, "A serious attempt to address the issue of a reduction in CO_2 emissions may raise wholesale electricity prices by up to 60 percent in five years."

The study noted, "No matter how large the wind power capacity, the variable nature of its output means it can make no significant contribution to security of energy supply."

Renewables Lobby Concedes Study's Accuracy

An association of renewable energy companies, Scottish Renewables, conceded in a written response published in *The Scotsman* that the Hume Institute study accurately reflected the annual costs of supplying power through renewable sources. The renewable energy association also conceded, "Because of the cost of providing additional stand-by generating capacity, it is unlikely wind power will ever account for more than 20 percent of electricity generation through the National Grid, and will make no substantial contribution to a reduction in carbon emissions."

"The government should take advantage of the renewables review coming up in 2005–6 to reconsider the nuclear option," wrote Simpson. "Nuclear power avoids extra costs, emits no greenhouse gases, and contributes to security of supply."

Analysts Note Environmental Consequences

Analysts noted economic costs are not the only costs associated with wind power. Many environmentalists oppose wind power because of the substantial number of birds slaughtered by turbine blades every year. In Northern California's Altamont Pass wind fields alone, thousands of birds are killed by wind turbines each year, including roughly 1,000 annual kills of such valued birds of prey as golden eagles, red-tailed hawks, and burrowing owls.

Property owners near turbine locations also oppose wind power because of sight and sound pollution. The size of a single turbine tower and the large number of such turbines necessary to generate any measurable amount of electricity destroy any esthetic beauty of the turbine location, and the cumulative noise of the turbines is, report nearby residents, often unbearable.

"Wind power may well be the least environmentally friendly idea ever proposed by environmentalists," noted Iain Murray, a senior fellow at the Competitive Enterprise Institute. "Conservationists as committed as Sen. Edward Kennedy (D-Massachusetts) and British television personality Dr. David Bellamy have come out against proposed uses of the technology."

In addition to environmental concerns, new evidence suggests wind turbines may be contributing to human disease such as malaria and West Nile Virus spread by mosquitoes.

The American Wind Energy Association (AWEA) conceded in a recent press release that wind turbines are frequently killing bats that cannot detect or avoid the turbines. Acknowledged the AWEA, "Wind power providers found bats fatally collided with turbines in West Virginia, Tennessee, Minnesota, and Wyoming last year. Bats play an important role as primary predators of night flying insects, including many major agricultural pests, and they pollinate plants and disperse seeds."

Organic Farming Is Good for the Environment

Jonathan Dimbleby

About the author: Jonathan Dimbleby is a British journalist and broadcaster.

A few years ago [in the late nineties] few bothered about the organic movement except to mock the Prince of Wales [Prince Charles] for his pioneering contribution to what has now become a major debate about the crops we grow and the food we eat. Today [in 2001], however, the organic movement is on a roller-coaster; the number of people who choose to grow or consume organic produce is rising at a dramatic rate, a phenomenon that is forcing everyone involved at every stage in the food chain to rethink the basic assumptions of the last 50 years.

Yet despite this growth, this rapid reassessment of recent agricultural developments, the organic movement has its critics and they are loud and insistent. 'Organic farming cannot feed an ever-increasing global population,' they shout; 'It cannot weather the inconsistencies of climate', they continue; and they conclude with the ever-common mantra: 'It's just too expensive'.

The critics of the organic movement have much to say, and before I continue, I must be honest. There was once a time when I may have been among their number.

Pesticides to the Rescue

I was brought up on a small farm in Sussex. I took it all for granted. The cats, the dogs, the ponies, the cows, the pigs, the chickens and two geese ominously named Christmas Day and Boxing Day who grew very old and fierce—because, when the

Jonathan Dimbleby, "Down on the Farm," *The Ecologist*, vol. 3, February 2001, p. 44. Copyright © 2001 by MIT Press Journals. Reproduced by permission.

moment arrived, no-one had had the temerity to take the action required to turn them into a feast. On our farm, chemical fertilisers were still a novelty, referred to disparagingly as 'artificial'. Pesticides, similarly, were unknown: docks, nettles and thistles were scythed away by hand just as they came into seed. Antibiotics were a last resort, not an addiction. We did not use the term organic; indeed I had never heard of it.

I decided I wanted to be a farmer. I went to agricultural college and remember trying to create on paper a profitable farm business. I soon discovered that it was—apparently— impossible both to make money and to recreate the traditional character of my childhood acres. The figures simply didn't stack up. To succeed, I discovered, you had to specialise.

You needed vast acres of corn or an intensive dairy farm with scores if not hundreds of cows—thin and spindly creatures, invariably black and white in colour with pendulous udders, designed and constructed by geneticists to produce vast quantities of milk in the most efficient way possible.

Or you could have battery chickens in their hundreds of thousands, caged and cramped to prevent them moving around freely and thus expending wasteful energy that should be more profitably deployed either laying an egg a day or getting fat as fast as possible. Or pigs, sows tethered in stalls, piglets weaned early and reared in the semi-dark on wooden slats in a humid atmosphere that reeked of dung and urine. It was a world in which farmers were required to be permanently at war—zapping the enemy that lurked in the soil, in the hedges, trees and ponds, in the very air itself, with an awesome selection of chemical firepower. Victory would be secured with pesticides, herbicides, and fungicides. And, in the case of livestock, with the wonder of antibiotics used on a daily basis both to promote growth and to prevent disease.

It was a brave new world and it was remarkably seductive. Food would be plentiful and cheap and we would all live happily ever after. I bought the argument hook, line and sinker. I even wrote an article which was published in the college magazine suggesting that the vista was not only attractive but exceedingly profitable. And I castigated the farming community for moaning all the way to the bank with their huge subsidy cheques from the British taxpayer.

Environmental Devastation on a Global Scale

Anyway, I soon found myself on another primrose path. Via university and into television where I spent a great deal of time travelling the world from one crisis or disaster to another. In India, Latin America, but especially in Africa, and there, particularly in Ethiopia, I saw the horrific consequences of what were then widely regarded as natural disasters. The rains failing; the droughts; the seed perishing on the stalk; no grain. People starving.

It was a world in which farmers were. . .zapping the enemy that lurked in the soil, in the hedges, trees and ponds . . . with an awesome selection of chemical firepower.

In Ethiopia in 1973, I stumbled across human suffering on a scale that I could scarcely believe. People dead and dying on the roadside and in makeshift camps in the towns and villages round about. I saw piles of bodies waiting to be buried; entire families; mothers and fathers, children and tiny babies. To witness such things—a young mother grieving for the dead baby she still clasped to her chest—reminded me of the concentration camp at Belsen [Germany], the full horror of which was revealed to the world in 1945 by my father. No-one thought that Belsen was a natural disaster: everyone knew that it was the calculated consequence of an evil vision.

It seemed to me that this first famine in Ethiopia, or rather the first to attract a huge international response—whilst very different from the crime against humanity perpetrated at

Belsen—was not possible to explain away, glibly and forgivingly, as a natural disaster.

Essential to the idea of organic production is the belief that it is possible to work with nature, not against nature.

It is true that the rains had failed. But the soil was also eroding fast. Trees and forests had been cut down to provide fuel and even the most fertile soils were eroding at an alarming rate. Water storage and irrigation systems were notable by their absence. And it was also noticeable that only the poor succumbed while the rich—the landowners, the merchants, the officials, the ministers and the generals—continued to prosper.

So I met people who knew better, and I read, and I learnt a little. And as a result I came to the view that almost no disaster was natural—and that the environmental devastation was both cause and effect: the product of a complex set of interwoven causes—among the most obvious of which were poverty, injustice, corruption, repression and war. A vicious circle and a vortex for hundreds of millions of innocent people.

Sustainable Development Needs Organic Production

To put it another way: we must treat the planet as if we are going to live for ever and not as though we had simply dropped in for a weekend break. I think that is a pretty good rule of thumb, litmus test and guide to action. The phrase used today to describe this approach is 'sustainable development'.

What I've seen in the poorest parts of the poorest countries of the Third World over the last 25 years offers a crucial challenge to the notion of sustainable development. You cannot have sustainable development anywhere on earth when the great majority of the global population is getting poorer while the rest of us get richer. That is a recipe for disaster, not development. If it is to mean anything at all, sustainable development must be about fairness in the use of the resources on which we all depend for survival.

And that, for me, is where sustainable development meets the organic movement. Essential to the idea of organic production is the belief that it is possible to work with nature, not against nature. That you can produce high quality and nutritious food without zapping every predator in sight. That good timing and sensible crop rotation, combined with a respect for bio-diversity, is the most sustainable form of agriculture possible: protecting the environment, enhancing human health, and—incidentally—strengthening, not weakening, the social and economic fabric of rural communities.

All Species Are Interdependent

Organic production is based on the principle that, in the chain of life on earth, no species is irrelevant and all are interdependent: from bacteria to fungi, from insects to vertebrates. Adherence to organic principles requires respect for these intricate relationships that between them sustain the biosphere— and thereby human existence.

A measure of that intricacy is the fact that if you scoop up one cubic metre of earth from an ancient beech forest, you will find no fewer than 50,000 small earthworms, 50,000 insects and mites, and 12 million roundworms. From one gramme of that soil you might unearth some 30,000 protozoa, 50,000 algae, 400,000 fungi and billions of individual bacteria of unknown species.

The American poet, farmer and philosopher, Wendell Berry, writes of this organic life in the soil in lyrical, almost spiritual, terms:

'The soil is the healer and restorer and resurrector by which disease passes into health, age into youth, death into life. Without proper care for it we can have no community, because without proper care for it we can have no life.

'It is alive itself. It is a grave, too, of course. Or a healthy soil is. It is full of dead animals and plants, bodies that have passed through other bodies... the only way into the soil is through other bodies. But no matter how finely the dead are broken down, or how many times they are eaten, they yet give in to other life. If a healthy soil is full of death it is also full of life... Given only the health of the soil nothing that dies is dead for very long.'

The Prince of Wales is fond of saying that seeing is believing. And when you see organic crops in the field, you know what he means. I have seen a field of beans, black and sticky with aphids. You think that the crop must be doomed. And then three months later the aphids have entirely disappeared. And the crop looks wonderful.

What has happened? No, not a drop of pesticide. No dust from any fungicide. The work has been done by ladybirds [ladybugs]. Ladybirds which have come into life in the surrounding hedgerows, protected in a chemical-free environment and, as nature dictates, moved in en masse to wipe out the aphids and clean up the crop. It happens year after year. Natural predation; no chemicals.

Protecting Biodiversity

In this context, I am a touch perplexed by Sir John Krebs, the new head of the Food Standards Agency [in England] who seems to me to have been rather less well-advised than might have been good for him. How can he be so certain as to instruct the public—as he did on a recent BBC *Countryfile* programme—that consumers are wasting their money if they think they are getting extra safety by buying organic? Why is he so dismissive? I am sure that he has not been nobbled [that is, co-opted by an opposing group]. Yet he has allowed himself to rush into judgement.

A growing body of research demonstrates that the beneficial effects of organic farming in protecting biodiversity go much wider. Indeed, there is evidence to show what organic producers have long suspected: that organic farming methods are an exceptionally effective way of protecting the wildlife of rural Britain.

For my own part, I end almost where I started—with thoughts of local farming, and my own process of learning. I once thought that intensive farming was the way ahead—the more you grow, the more you feed; everyone's happy. But in those young years of mine I was viewing agriculture in an isolated context, failing to see that farms are not just providers of food, but intrinsic human relationships with the world around us all. The more I read and saw, the more the bigger picture began to reveal itself.

For me, organic agriculture is destined to play a crucial part in that big picture: helping to create a future in which those who follow us—our children and our children's children—will be able to look back and say, 'they did us proud'.

Genetically Modified Crops Benefit the Environment More than Organic Foods Do

The San Diego Center for Molecular Agriculture

About the author: The San Diego Center for Molecular Agriculture is an alliance of scientists working at public research institutions in San Diego.

By the year 2050 there are likely to be 9 billion people on this Earth, an increase of 50 percent over the present day. Most of this increase will occur in the cities of developing countries, primarily in Asia. If present economic development continues, this population increase will require a doubling in food production. Only a fraction of the food that all these people will need can be produced in the breadbaskets of the world. Most of this food has to be grown locally. The problem of feeding all the people is worsened by the uneven distribution of cropland. For example, China has a quarter of the human population but only 7 percent of the world's farmland.

During the last doubling of the human population from 3 billion in 1960 to 6 billion in 2000, food production increases kept up with population growth because we created and adopted multiple new technologies. Better techniques to cultivate the soil, new irrigation technologies, more advanced pesticides that are biodegradable, better genetic strains, machinery that harvests more of the crop, synthetic fertilizers, and green manures that restore the nutrients to the soil all have helped raise food production.

GM Crops Are Only Part of the Answer

GM [genetically modified] crops are not the magic bullet that

San Diego Center for Molecular Agriculture, "Foods from Genetically Modified Crops," San Diego, CA: San Diego Center for Molecular Agriculture. Copyright © by the San Diego Center for Molecular Agriculture. Reproduced by permission.

will feed the world. But they can certainly help because they are an integral part of our continuing quest for the genetic improvement of crops. We can't afford to reject this technology as some are advocating. Progress must be made in other technologies as well. We need more durable, longer-lasting disease and insect resistance, irrigation systems that waste less water, agronomic systems with multiple crops that limit erosion on sloping land. We need to find out which types of soil tilling, fertilizer application, and crop rotation produce the healthiest soils with the most beneficial microbial activity. We need to learn so many things, and yet financial support for agricultural research has been slowly eroding for twenty years.

GM crops cannot eliminate poverty and hunger because these problems are rooted in the socio-political realm. People need jobs to purchase food and with economic demand food production usually picks up. Although the world does indeed produce enough food to eliminate hunger, we have not yet devised an economic system that permits the distribution of that food in an equitable way.

Technologies are not an unmitigated blessing, especially when they are first introduced. Cars pollute the air and people are killed in accidents, but few people want to be without an automobile. Agricultural technologies also have negative effects. To make them better requires our human ingenuity. President Jimmy Carter said it so well: "Responsible biotechnology is not the enemy; starvation is."

Manipulating Crops

We are all familiar with the glorious sight of a full ear of ripe sweet corn, but what does the ear of the ancestor of the corn plant look like? Some 6,000 to 8,000 years ago Native Americans in Mexico began the slow process of domesticating teosinte, the ancestor of corn. Teosinte still grows wild in Mexico. It produces tiny "ears" with very small seeds, each contained in a tough thick husk, that fall on the ground when they are dry. The plant itself also does not look like a modern corn plant with its single tall stalk, because the species was genetically modified through the intervention of humans. Corn probably has as many as 25,000 different genes and we have no idea how many have been mutated, deleted, rearranged, or duplicated in the past 5,000 years of human manipulation. All these genetic modifications are to our advantage because an acre of corn yields 1,000 times more food than an acre of teosinte.

As you travel through the countryside, whether in Mexico, Iowa, Kenya, or Italy, all corn-growing regions, you never see corn growing outside of a field or garden. That's because corn cannot survive without our assistance. It is a natural plant, but it can't survive in nature!

What is true of corn is also true of our other food crops: wheat, rice, beans, and soybeans were all genetically modified and can't survive on their own. Crop domestication, the process of changing wild plants to crop plants, started in south China and the Middle East about 10,000 years ago and in west Africa and central Mexico 8,000 years ago.

Organic farmers and opponents of genetic engineering accept such varieties as 'natural.' However, they consider the next innovation in breeding, which uses molecular techniques, to be 'unnatural.'

At the start of the twentieth century, farmers and breeders started improving crops more systematically. First they simply worked in the field, making crosses and producing hybrids from plants of the same species. Starting about 1950, breeders began experimenting with wide hybridization: crossing different species and rescuing the tiny embryos through laboratory culture (otherwise, the embryos die because the plants are of unrelated species). To produce a crop from such a cross does require many generations of plant breeding. A major new cereal called triticale was produced in this way by crossing wheat and rye.

Then came radiation breeding. Seeds were irradiated with gamma rays—which knock the DNA for a loop—and the plants with their damaged DNA were crossed back to healthy plants. The idea was—and this proved to be correct—that some changes in the DNA would prove to be beneficial to the farmer. In this, as in all plant breeding, extensive crossing (six to ten generations) eliminates all the "bad" DNA and keeps only the "good" DNA. Chemicals have also been used to induce mutations. Hundreds of crop varieties are now in use that were produced by these methods. Organic farmers and opponents of genetic engineering accept such varieties as "natural." However, they consider the next innovation in breeding, which uses molecular techniques, to be "unnatural."

The problem is that certified organic farming is driven by ideology, not by sound science or even a 'love of the land.'

Is Organic Farming the Answer?

Certified organic farming is defined as much by what it does not accept as by what it does accept. For most of its farming practices it turns the clock back to 1950 and disavows the use of all but a few pesticides (such as rotenone, which is actually quite poisonous), and rejects all herbicides and most inorganic (chemical) fertilizers. It prefers organic fertilizers (manure), mechanical removal of weeds (with tractors), and biological pest control. It accepts all methods of producing improved crop plants (including radiation breeding) but rejects GM crops that use gene transfer. Organic farming can feed about 3 billion people, not the 6 billion that we now have, or the 9 billion that we will have.

Why is this so? There are several reasons, according to Professor Tony Trewavas, an eminent British plant biologist and fellow of the Royal Society of Great Britain. First of all, to produce the manure necessary to raise the organic crops, a considerable amount of land must be set aside to raise food for the animals. Secondly, crop harvesting and food consumption result in a net transfer of plant nutrients from the soil to the toilets of city dwellers! Replacement of these nutrients through crop rotations with legumes and by utilizing rock phosphate is imperfect at best. Also, biological control of insects and diseases is not as efficient as chemical control or control by genetic modification in many crops. These factors all conspire to make organic farming less efficient and certified organic produce more expensive than traditional farming.

However, there are many positive aspects to organic farming that are practiced by many farmers. Crop rotations with legumes, the use of crop residues to improve the soil, integrated or biological pest control when appropriate, and use of lime to change the acidity of the soil are just a few examples of practices that are part of "sustainable" agriculture. The problem is that certified organic farming is driven by ideology, not by sound science or even a "love of the land." Organic farmers reject technologies that other farmers incorporate in their cropland management schemes to achieve a sustainable form of agriculture. Scientists who support GM crops agree that farming must be made more sustainable, but reject the ideology-driven approach of organic farmers.

Preserving Wilderness Requires Increased Crop Productivity

For some 5000 years, crop production has been reshaping our landscape. Forests have been cleared and prairies plowed under. The landscape may still be pleasing to the eye—vineyards in California, olive groves in Spain, rice paddies in Malaysia—but the diversity of plants and animals that characterized earlier times has been lost. Not because of GM crops, but because of our need to feed an ever-growing human population coupled with our inability to increase productivity (yield per acre) fast enough. This means that ever-increasing amounts of land have had to be put to the plow.

The results are plenty of food for 90 percent of the human population—100 percent if we could distribute it equitably—and a litany of problems: loss of species diversity, soil erosion, and salt build-up. The spread of weeds and pathogens from one continent to another and the emergence of new insect pests also result from the intensification of agriculture. But none of these problems exist because of GM crops.

We need to do much better! We need to make agriculture more sustainable so that at least some of these problems can be partially alleviated. Increasing sustainability and raising productivity will tax our human ingenuity to the limit.

It is odd that environmentalists who rightfully lament the loss of biodiversity are not taking a strong position in favor of technologies that can raise agricultural productivity. Indeed, there is a clear link between crop productivity and the maintenance of biodiversity.

All the good land and much marginal land is already being cultivated. What is left is even more marginal: poorer soils or drier climates, fields higher on the slopes of mountains. If we push production into those areas the damage to the environment will be greater. So, if we want to preserve wilderness lands and the biodiversity they offer, we have to increase crop productivity on agricultural lands. GM technologies can make a real contribution to this goal. The GM crops already in the fields require fewer pesticide applications and less tilling of the soil—thereby causing less erosion. Most importantly, we need to increase productivity. If doubling food production will require us to double the cultivated area, there would be no wilderness left. Let's bring all our knowledge and all our technologies—simple and sophisticated—to bear on the important issue of making agriculture more productive and environmentally friendly.

Making Sport Utility Vehicles More Efficient Would Help Conserve the Environment

Gregg Easterbrook

About the author: Gregg Easterbrook is a senior editor at the New Republic, a weekly opinion journal.

[The fall 2002] sniper attacks in Montgomery County, Maryland, created gridlock outside public schools, as many parents responded by driving their children each morning. Sitting in the paralyzed traffic around my children's middle school during that period, intersections in three directions blocked by queues of metal, I beheld what modern transportation trends have wrought. At least half the machines jockeying for position at the drop-off point were some form of "sport utility vehicle" (SUV)—a clear mirror of buying trends, since SUVs and deceptively named "light" pickup trucks now represent half of new-vehicle sales. Many of the SUVs were huge, twice the size of regular four-door cars. Drivers of the SUVs were usually the aggressive ones, trying to barge to the front and cut off the cars of people who were, after all, the parents of their kids' friends at school.

What I observed, facing the tonnage of automotive sheet metal lined up outside Cabin John Middle School in this suburban haven, represented twenty years of public-policy fiasco. Perverse federal regulations have actually encouraged auto companies to make SUVs big and wasteful, creating the very emblem of contemporary selfishness. Special congressional exemptions permit the vehicles to emit far more smog-forming pollutants and greenhouse gases than regular cars. Safety loopholes allow SUVs to be more dangerous than regular cars: it is

Gregg Easterbrook, "Axle of Evil—America's Twisted Love Affair with Sociopathic Cars," *The New Republic*, January 20, 2003. Copyright © 2003 by The New Republic, Inc. Reproduced by permission.

a common fallacy that the occupants inside SUVs are safer than they would be in ordinary cars, and these Godzillas are instruments of death for non-SUV-driving motorists. Advertising has created the illusion that owning an SUV has something to do with being outdoorsy and adventurous, yet hardly any of these vehicles are used off-road, and the kind of four-wheel-drive systems that many sport to maintain the off-road fiction are nearly worthless in normal driving conditions, and even in snow. Still other perverse special favors have allowed SUVs to have blackout windows, mammoth grill guards, dazzling headlights, and other features designed to make the vehicles as aggressive and hostile as possible.

To top off the scandal, the petroleum-waste trends caused by the SUV and its cousin, the light pickup (which is also exempt from most safety and environmental rules for regular cars, though millions of supposedly commercial-purpose pickups are used as cars), keep American society perilously dependent on Persian Gulf oil, diverting $20 billion annually to Saudi Arabia and its anti-American extremists, and $10 billion annually to [then Iraqi dictator] Saddam Hussein himself. Stuck in the school-bound traffic, I marveled at the absurdity of our national situation. The country was preparing to make war with Saddam partly over his oil, and here was a parade of SUVs brazenly attesting to the rarely discussed fact that American gasoline stations are Saddam's financial benefactor. Every time an SUV or light pickup leaves the showroom in the United States, fanatics smile in the Persian Gulf. . . .

SUVs Are Allowed to Emit More Pollutants

Americans have always loved large cars—well, almost always, and this brings us to the birth of the SUV. Following the oil crunch in 1973, gasoline was much more expensive in real-dollar terms than it is today, and Congress imposed fuel-economy standards on passenger vehicles. These factors combined with Detroit's severe quality-control problems of the

1970s and the advent of high-quality Toyotas, Hondas, and Datsuns to make smaller cars fashionable during the late 1970s and early 1980s. Buyers were abandoning land yachts for nimble small or mid-size vehicles. Detroit needed a new large-vehicle product to help reverse its declining market share.

Every SUV and light pickup sold in the United States is allowed to emit substantially more smog-forming pollutants than regular cars.

At about the same time, the old American Motors company was making a push to market its Jeep brand as a vehicle for everyone, not just for backwoodsmen. The company was in financial trouble. [Journalist Keith] Bradsher reports that its lobbyists told officials of Richard Nixon's newly created Environmental Protection Agency (EPA) that if the company went under, they would blame the anti-pollution rules of the newly passed Clean Air Act. So the EPA wrote a waiver that essentially exempted Jeeps from anti-smog regulation, on the grounds that they were not cars but "light trucks." That trucks should get a pass on clean-air rules was itself something of an absurdity. Ostensibly the provision was to protect business, but since the deadweight cost of pollution control is the same from the standpoint of the economy regardless of whether the price is imposed on individuals or on businesses, the distinction never made much sense. In any event, Jeeps were issued a free pass.

You can guess what followed. Other manufacturers demanded free passes for anything even vaguely truckish, including light pickups. Automakers rushed to create a new class of large vehicles with obscure design elements (such as the option of ordering a model with panel sides instead of rear side windows) that allowed manufacturers to claim that they were trucks, even if they were plainly intended for use as cars. To this day, every SUV and light pickup sold in the United

States is allowed to emit substantially more smog-forming pollutants than regular cars. Dramatic action against this problem was supposedly taken during the [Bill] Clinton administration—but the dramatic action in question was to extend the free pass to the year 2009, when SUVs finally, at least in theory, must meet anti-pollution standards.

SUVs Could Meet Anti-Pollution Rules

All the decent people who buy SUVs in the conviction that they are safe or chic should recognize that their vehicles are pollution-spewing hogs. Regular cars, for which anti-pollution controls are extremely strict, get cleaner every year, so much so that smog should be declining rapidly in most cities. But smog decline has slowed in the last decade, and the reason is the SUV. The Washington, D.C., metropolitan area, for example, was expected ten years ago to be off the EPA smog-problem list by now because the trend in pollution from regular cars was sharply down; but so many smog-emitting SUVs have invaded the area, bringing their anti-pollution exemptions with them, that in the last few years the quality of local air has actually declined.

This decline is not because it is impossible to build a clean-running engine that delivers enough power for a large vehicle. The big engines of some modern full-size cars, such as certain Cadillacs, run with hardly any smog emissions. The 240-horsepower V-6 engine of my family's Honda Odyssey minivan, built in Alabama, generates enough power to move an SUV, but it emits barely measurable pollutants, less than 10 percent of the amount allowed by the standard for regular cars, which is already quite strict. SUV and light pickup engines that could meet anti-pollution rules would be wholly practical. It is just that they are not required, so Detroit does not build them; and Congress, which is in Detroit's pocket, keeps putting off the day when the requirement will kick in.

To strengthen its argument that the first SUV versions of Jeeps were really trucks—even though the company was loading them with luxury features for marketing as personal cars—American Motors pointed to the Jeep's truck-like undercarriage and to its purported ability to operate off-road.

Eventually a federal bureaucrat decreed that an SUV with air conditioning, leather seats, and other suburban amenities becomes a truck if it is "capable of off-highway operation." The test of this, in turn, became whether the vehicle is tall enough to provide ground clearance. So Detroit made the early SUVs very tall, to be assured of the pollution-control exemption. Height makes SUVs hostile-looking, causes their headlights to dazzle oncoming drivers, makes them block other drivers' view of the road, and renders them more likely to roll over. But it assures the exemption, which was all that mattered.

The Rules Reward Waste

Detroit deliberately made SUVs heavier and more wasteful. In the 1970s, as the rules of the Clean Air Act took force, federal mileage standards also went into effect. An asterisk in the rules specified that they did not apply to vehicles in excess of 6,000 pounds gross weight (vehicle weight plus maximum load). This asterisk was intended to keep the miles-per-gallon (MPG) rules for regular cars from affecting real trucks, since at the time there were no ordinary vehicles with a gross weight in excess of 6,000 pounds. But early SUV manufacturers realized that if they beefed up the suspensions of their products to reach the 6,000-pound mark, they could evade mileage restrictions. So Detroit deliberately made SUVs heavier and more wasteful. The rules, you see, had been set up to reward waste.

By the 1990s, a federal "fleet" standard (the average of all new models sold by a manufacturer) of 20.7 miles per gallon would be established for SUVs, versus the federal standard of

27.5 miles per gallon for regular cars. But though cars as a group actually meet the federal mileage requirement, the SUV standard remains shot through with loopholes. Manufacturers get exemptions if they declare SUVs "dual fuel," or capable of running on ethanol. Millions of SUVs and pickups are now "dual fuel" for rule-evasion purposes, though almost none actually run on ethanol. (In most states, gas stations do not even sell ethanol.) Federal MPG ratings are also derived from unrealistic tests in which SUVs are daintily accelerated with air conditioners off and never, ever driven above the speed limit—since speeding, as we know, is illegal.

Detroit deliberately made SUVs heavier and more wasteful.

Officially, the Dodge Durango gets 13 miles per gallon in city driving and scores just 1 on the 1-to-10 EPA scale of clean-air performance. The Chevy Avalanche gets 13 miles per gallon in the city and scores 0 on a scale of 10. The Cadillac Escalade gets 12 miles per gallon and hits 0 on a scale of 10. The Chevy Tahoe—owned by Leonardo DiCaprio, who demands that everyone else sacrifice to prevent an artificial greenhouse effect—gets 14 miles per gallon and 0 on a scale of 10 for environmental responsibility. And in actual use drivers will be lucky to realize even these pathetically low figures.

Low mileage in SUVs and pickups is not dictated by the laws of nature any more than pollution-spewing is. Automotive engineers, including those in Detroit, have accomplished wonders with MPG improvement. Full-sized cars such as the Ford Crown Victoria and Chevy Impala now do well on an MPG basis. The new Impala records 32 MPG on the highway, a number that Toyota and Datsun buyers would have envied in the 1970s. The large Buick Park Avenue gets 20 miles per gallon in the city and earns a 7 on the environmental scale of

10. Detroit knows perfectly well how to build fuel-efficient, low-polluting large vehicles.

SUVs Granted Special Waivers

Large cars now do well on fuel efficiency because the MPG rules for regular cars are actually enforced, compelling Detroit to comply. But Congress has repeatedly granted special waivers for SUVs: in 1990, in a showdown during which a Senate filibuster was used to block progress, and again in 2002, when a bill to improve SUV and pickup mileage drew only 38 votes in the Senate. (Even many Democrats voted nay.) Just before Christmas, President George W. Bush announced that SUV and light pickup fuel-efficiency standards would rise about 10 percent, to an official fleet average of 22.2 MPG, by the model year 2007. Ten percent improvement is preferable to inaction, but it is far less than the SUV fuel efficiency gains that the National Research Council recently told the White House would be practical using current technology. Also, the administration's decision leaves the "dual fuel" gimmick in place, meaning that many SUVs and pickups will simply evade the new standard.

> Large cars now do well on fuel efficiency because the MPG rules for regular cars are actually enforced. . . . But Congress has repeatedly granted special waivers for SUVs.

Why such resistance to improving fuel efficiency for SUVs? Since SUVs and light pickups are now Detroit's most profitable products—owing to their popularity, they command price premiums and sell at considerable mark-ups—an unholy alliance of conservatives who oppose federal energy-efficiency rules and Democrats from United Automobile Workers (UAW) states consistently blocks legislative attempts to do nothing more radical than require SUVs and pickups to meet the same standards as regular cars. Detroit does need profit; and, as

Bradsher writes, SUV revenues "have contributed to the economic revival of the upper Midwest." But SUVs would still be profitable if they were fuel-efficient, clean, and safe: and all three of those qualities are technologically attainable. The only vehicle type that would be put out of existence by meaningfully higher mileage standards would be the ultra-offensive Excursion, Tahoe, and Hummer class of leviathan SUVs, the existence of which represents a classic "public nuisance" in legal terms anyway.

Making Sport Utility Vehicles More Efficient Would Not Benefit the Environment

Barry McCahill

About the author: Barry McCahill is the president of the Sport Utility Vehicle Owners of America, a group devoted to preserving the rights of SUV owners.

Sport Utility Vehicle Owners of America (SUVOA) is a national non-profit organization representing the interests of the nation's more than 26 million SUV owners, including 3.4 million in California.

SUVOA Communications Director Ron DeFore commented in person at the July 7, 2004 California Air Resources Board (ARB) Public Workshop, providing our view on pending regulations to implement Assembly Bill 1493 (AB 1493).[1] Since the workshop, we expect you may have heard from another SUVOA emissary, "Squeezy the Clown," whom we employed as a mechanism to attract public attention to this arcane yet enormously damaging proposed policy. Our written testimony today poses several pivotal questions that require your serious and specific response.

CO_2 Is Not a Toxic Pollutant

All Americans want to do their part for the environment and support efforts to encourage vehicles that are safer, cleaner and more fuel efficient. But average citizens are understandably confused by the complexities and discourse involving environmental public policy—a perplexity that serves those who

---

1. This bill seeks to reduce carbon dioxide and other greenhouse gases from passenger vehicles. It was passed on July 1, 2002.

Barry McCahill, testimony before the California Air Resources Board. September, 23, 2004.

wish to advance an agenda that would never fly if the public were more cognizant of the ultimate benefits and tradeoffs.

To that point, ARB has a responsibility to make sure that CO_2 is not portrayed even subtly as a toxic pollutant, even though ARB has chosen to label it a pollutant. Most people equate the word "pollutant" with toxic substances, which does not apply to CO_2, a naturally occurring compound that is essential both to plants and animals.

It is incumbent upon ARB to fully disclose to California residents the realistic implications of the regulatory policy it is poised to implement. While ballyhooed by some as "cleaner air, environmental leadership with no downsides," the reality is this: SUVs and other light trucks would become much more expensive and less useful for towing and hauling. What's more, because climate change involves all nations, what California does with this proposed regulation would provide absolutely no measurable environmental benefit. And possibly some harm, as noted below.

There is no feasible chemical or mechanical process (like a catalytic converter) that can be applied to tailpipe emissions to reduce CO_2. Even proponents of this regulation recognize that the only viable CO_2 reduction technique is to burn less fuel. In turn, the only ways to reduce fuel consumption is to restrict driving or demand greater vehicle fuel economy. Since AB 1493 explicitly prohibits the first approach (following the state's seismic misadventures with mandatory trip reduction strategies during the previous decade), fuel economy enhancement is the only alternative. But doing so involves significant trade-offs that the public needs to know about *now*—not when the resulting vehicles are offered for sale many years hence.

Faulty Regulations

While we sympathize with ARB's dilemma in attempting to implement AB 1493, the law contains several contradictory and unrealistic statements to reassure Californians that this is a "no-cost, side-effect-free" action, when history flatly proves that will not be the case.

Specifically, AB 1493 states the regulations "shall not require any of the following" :

- "Imposition of additional fees on any motor vehicle."

!?!? How does this language square with the reality that increases in fuel efficiency needed to achieve CO_2 reductions must come either from lighter vehicles or using more expensive materials/technologies? Or is the use of the term "fee" meant to distract consumers from the fact that they will pay additional costs, whether or not it is in the form of a "fee" assessed by the State of California?

- "The ban on the sale of any vehicle category in the state, specifically including, but not limited to sport utility vehicles and light-duty trucks."

!?!? To reiterate, CO_2-reducing fuel efficiency gains necessarily must come either from down-sizing vehicles or making them more expensive. While an overt ban may not be implemented, this appears to be sheer trickery of the public. We won't "ban" your vehicle category, but our regulation will make it unrecognizable from its current form just as federal Corporate Average Fuel Economy standards in the 1970s and 1980s drove large family station wagons into extinction. Ironically but informatively, the unavailability of large, useful station wagons is a key reason for why SUVs have become a mainstay of California families. This language seems to be another shell-game palliative for the vehicle-buying public.

- "A reduction in vehicle weight."

!?!? Our unavoidable mantra again: CO_2-reducing fuel efficiency gains inherently rely on down-weighting vehicles or using more expensive materials/technologies. If Bullet #1 is true, then Bullet #3 must be false or vice versa as defined by AB

1493's language that the regulations "shall not require ANY of the following" [emphasis added].

SUVOA urges ARB, California legislators and the current administration to level with the public. It you possess the magic means to occasion a 25 percent jump in fuel efficiency (and corresponding 25 percent reduction in CO_2 emissions) with virtually no side effects, then share it with the public and do so in specific detail. Or if you know of ways by which CO_2 can realistically and affordably be reduced without forcing drastic fuel economy reductions, show us how, again in specific detail. For if not, owners of SUVs and other practical vehicles will have no choice but to hold you responsible for not disclosing the dramatic side-effects detailed below.

Reducing Vehicle Weight Is Dangerous

Let us be clear: SUVOA strongly supports efforts to improve motor vehicle fuel efficiency and reduce truly harmful emissions—twin goals that are being accomplished with every passing model year, but in a way that does not restrict consumer vehicle choices or work against vehicle performance and utility. But increasing fuel economy beyond affordable technologies to scrub CO_2 that is not even defined as a pollutant would force design changes that would lead to more injuries or deaths, and/or power train compromises that would have dramatically adverse consequences on business and recreational vehicle users.

Your requirement would usher in another round of vehicle down-sizing to trim weight to increase miles-per-gallon performance. This process has a long and bloody history, proven by numerous credible studies. The laws of physics are enforced with brutal clarity when vehicles collide. All things held equal, smaller vehicles offer less crash protection than larger ones.

Irresponsibly, AB 1493 puts more weight on computer models of global climate change (some of which cannot even replicate what actually took place during a given forecasted period even after conditions forecasted during that period did not come to pass) than numerous reports demonstrating that mandated fuel economy requirements resulted in tens of thousands of additional lives lost. Every independent study of this issue by the federal government, respected independent organizations and the news media has reached the same conclusion of carnage. As one example, *USA Today* headlined its exhaustive 1999 investigative report on this subject, "Death by the Gallon."

SUVOA strongly supports efforts to improve motor vehicle fuel efficiency and reduce truly harmful emissions.

Researchers from the Harvard School of Public Health and the Brookings Institution estimated that vehicle downsizing in the late 1970s and early 1980s increased occupant deaths by 14 to 27 percent. Likewise, the National Highway Traffic Safety Administration (NHTSA) estimated that by 1993, down-sizing caused 1,300–2,600 deaths and 13,000 and 26,000 serious injuries per year above what would have occurred otherwise. A 2002 National Academy of Sciences study affirmed the NHTSA finding. A conservative tally of the death toll during the now more than quarter-century of federal fuel-economy regulation reveals that more than 50,000 Americans (more than 5,000 Californians) lost their lives because their down-sized vehicles provided less protection when they crashed.

The Difficulty in Reducing Federal Fuel Economy Standards

We believe the Assembly gave ARB an untenable assignment. In order to make the legislation more palatable politically, AB 1493 was packaged cleverly with many appealing caveats as noted above. It promises "technological solutions to reduce greenhouse gas emissions will stimulate the California economy and provide enhanced job opportunities," and predicts that the legislation will prevent wildfires and protect the State coastline from a rising sea level. To citizens reading news accounts on what is being proposed, it creates a harmless-sounding, "what's not to like?" scenario.

Glaringly missing from the debate is an honest and detailed discussion of what those supposed technological solutions are and whether or not they are marketable. If such automotive alchemy were so readily available and attractive to consumers, why wouldn't the ultra-competitive and self-interested auto industry long ago have employed it?

As testament to the difficulty of achieving fuel economy increases in a manner that is palatable to the vehicle-purchasing public, consider this: BMW paid a record $42 million in fines in 2003 for failing to meet federal fuel economy standards, one of several automakers who paid such fines. Why? In the words of a BMW spokesman, the German automaker paid the fines—which added more than $100 to the price of every vehicle sold—because the cost was regarded as a necessary evil in order to build "the cars our customers want to buy." Nor are federal fuel economy fines limited to high-performance vehicles: Volvo has a history of accepting the fuel economy fines and passing the added costs onto consumers in order to deliver the safer (but heavier) vehicles upon which its reputation is based.

There will be no free lunch in fulfilling this legislation. It will be pain without gain, with Californians sacrificing for an outcome even ARB has been unable to quantify. A far more productive course is to concentrate all energies on changes that will truly improve air quality and will truly reduce our reliance on foreign oil. A hydrogen economy potentially is one such course—a paradigm shift aggressively being pursued by [California] Governor [Arnold] Schwarzenegger, the auto and petroleum industries, among others.

Another example of AB 1493's divorce from reality is the bill's statement that implementing the law will "continue the California automobile worker tradition of building cars that use cutting edge technology." What tradition would that be? California has very little remaining auto manufacturing presence because of the State's staggering regulatory, tax and other government burdens, including higher labor costs than other western states. California accounts for approximately 12.8 percent of total US vehicle registration—but produces only 2.4 percent of new vehicles sold in America. If there were a capability to produce "cutting edge technology," why has your high-paid labor force not produced it already? Why not delay implementation of AB 1493 until California's automobile workers first demonstrate their "tradition" by solving the vexing technological challenges presented in this legislation?

Should ARB implement the proposed regulations, the results will be increased consumer costs for new vehicles; no positive influence on the earth's or California's environment; and trucks and SUVs (and luxury sedans for that matter) that are smaller, less safe, more expensive, and lacking many of the attributes that families, businesses and recreational enthusiasts need.

A far more productive course is to concentrate all energies on changes that will truly improve air quality and will truly reduce our reliance on foreign oil.

The ARB Plan Will Not Create Cleaner Air

The ARB plan likely would produce another unintended consequence: Dirtier air. Contrary to proponents who tout the regulation as a boon for clean air, higher new vehicle prices depress demand, meaning fewer new and cleaner vehicles would replace older, less clean models. California residents need to know a fact that is seldom reported—most of today's SUVs and other vehicles are 99 percent cleaner than their

1960s counterparts. A 2004 Chevy Suburban has stiffer ozone emission requirements than a 2000 Honda Civic.

Finally, California may, as stated in AB 1493, have "a long history of being the first in the nation to take action to protect public health and the environment." But it also has a similar history of forcing businesses and citizens to relocate out of the state because of oppressive government tax and regulatory burdens caused by trendy actions that lack any scientific basis. Has ARB even considered how it will deal with Californians who figure out a way to buy the inevitably less expensive new vehicles in other states just to import them back to California? Will another state agency be required to block frustrated Californians from seeking and using such loopholes? And with what impact on the state's cash-strapped coffers and the hundreds of new car dealers in California? Are ARB's major miscalculations during the 1990s with mandated employee trip reduction strategies and electric vehicles not instructive?

According to a recent article in the *San Francisco Chronicle*, "Discouraged by high costs and strict regulations, just under 60 percent of California business leaders interviewed said they have policies to restrict job growth in the state or move jobs to other locations in the United States." While some may want to thump their chests about environmental leadership, the study concluded, "California business regulations are more costly, complex and uncertain than those in any other state, by a wide margin." And all those costs are being borne by California consumers who in many cases probably would like less "leadership" on things of dubious value and more appreciation of the day-to-day financial challenges of working families and businesses.

ARB should send this bum piece of legislation back to the Assembly with a "No Can Do" stamp at the top, and with a cc to Governor Schwarzenegger, who pledged to rid the State of bad policy decisions precisely like this one.

Organizations to Contact

Cato Institute
1000 Massachusetts Ave. NW
  Washington, DC 20001-5403
(202) 842-0200 • fax: (202) 842-3490
e-mail: cato@cato.org
Web site: www.cato.org

The Cato Institute is a libertarian public policy research foundation dedicated to limiting the role of government and protecting individual liberties. The institute publishes the quarterly magazine *Regulation*, the bimonthly *Cato Policy Report*, and numerous books, including *Meltdown* and the *Cato Handbook of Policy*.

Competitive Enterprise Institute (CEI)
1001 Connecticut Ave. NW, Suite 1250
  Washington, DC 20036
(202) 331-1010 • fax: (202) 331-0640
e-mail: info@cei.org
Web site: www.cei.org

CEI encourages the use of free-market principles and private property rights to protect the environment. It advocates removing governmental regulatory barriers and establishing a system in which the private sector would be responsible for the environment. CEI's publications include the newsletter *Monthly Planet* and editorials in its On Point series, such as "What Every European Should Know About Global Warming."

Environmental Defense Fund
257 Park Ave. South, New York, NY 10010
(212) 505-2100 • fax: (212) 505-0892
e-mail: media@environmentaldefense.org
Web site: www.environmentaldefense.org

The fund is a public interest organization of lawyers, scientists, and economists dedicated to improvement of environmental quality and public health. It publishes brochures, fact sheets, and policy position papers.

Foundation for Clean Air Progress (FCAP)
1801 K St. NW, Suite 1000L
  Washington, DC 20036
(800) 272-1604
e-mail: info@cleanairprogress.org
Web site: www.cleanairprogress.org

FCAP is a nonprofit organization that believes the public is unaware of the progress that has been made in reducing air pollution. The foundation represents various sectors of business and industry in providing information to the public about improving air quality trends. FCAP publishes reports and studies demonstrating that air pollution is on the decline, including *Breathing Easier About Energy—a Healthy Economy and Healthier Air and Study on Air Quality Trends, 1970–2015*.

Foundation for Research on Economics and the Environment (FREE)
945 Technology Blvd., Suite 101F
  Bozeman, MT 59718
(406) 585-1776 • fax: (406) 585-3000
e-mail: jbaden@free-eco.org
Web site: free-eco.org

FREE is a research and education foundation committed to freedom, environmental quality, and economic progress. It works to reform environmental policy by using the principles of private property rights, the free market, and the rule of law. FREE publishes the quarterly newsletter *FREE Perspectives on Economics and the Environment* and produces a biweekly syndicated op-ed column.

Global Warming International Center (GWIC)
22W381 Seventy-fifth St.
  Naperville, IL 60565-9245
(630) 910-1551 • fax: (630) 910-1561
Web site: www.globalwarming.net

GWIC is an international body that provides information on global warming science and policy to industries and governmental and nongovernmental organizations. The center sponsors research supporting the understanding of global warming and ways to reduce the problem.

The Heritage Foundation
214 Massachusetts Ave. NE
  Washington, DC 20002
(202) 546-4400 • fax: (202) 546-8328
e-mail: info@heritage.org
Web site: www.heritage.org

The Heritage Foundation is a conservative think tank that supports the principles of free enterprise and limited government in environmental matters. Its many publications include "Improving the Endangered Species Act: Balancing the Needs of Landowners and Endangered Wildlife" and "Opening ANWR: Long Overdue."

National Audubon Society
700 Broadway, New York, NY 10003
(212) 979-3000 • fax: (212) 979-3188
e-mail: education@audubon.org
Web site: www.audubon.org

The society seeks to conserve and restore natural ecosystems, focusing on birds and other wildlife for the benefit of humanity and the earth's biological diversity. It publishes *Audubon* magazine and *WatchList*, which identifies North American bird species that are at risk of becoming endangered.

Natural Resources Defense Council (NRDC)
40 W. Twentieth St., New York, NY 10011
(212) 727-2700
e-mail: nrdcinfo@nrdc.org
Web site: www.nrdc.org

NRDC is an environmental group composed of lawyers and scientists who conduct research, work to educate the public, and lobby and litigate for environmental issues. The council publishes *Onearth* magazine as well as many books, pamphlets, brochures, and reports, many of which are available on its Web site.

Negative Population Growth, Inc. (NPG)
2861 Duke St., Suite 36
  Alexandria, VA 22314
(703) 370-9510 • fax: (703) 370-9514
e-mail: npg@npg.org
Web site: http://npg.org

NPG works to educate the American public and political leaders about the detrimental effects of overpopulation on the environment and quality of life. The organization advocates a smaller, more sustainable U.S. population accomplished through voluntary incentives for smaller families and limits on immigration. NPG publishes the quarterly newsletter *Population and Research Outlook* as well as many position papers and fact sheets.

Pew Center on Global Climate Change
2101 Wilson Blvd., Suite 550
  Arlington, VA 22201
(703) 516-4146 • fax: (703) 841-1422
Web site: www.pewclimate.org

The Pew Center is a nonpartisan organization dedicated to educating the public and policy makers about the causes and potential consequences of global climate change and informing them of ways to reduce the emissions of greenhouse gases. Its reports include *Reducing Transportation's Role in Climate Change*.

Political Economy Research Center (PERC)
2048 Analysis Dr., Bozeman, MT 59718
(406) 587-9591 • fax: (406) 586-7555
e-mail: perc@perc.org

Web site: www.perc.org

PERC is a research and education foundation that focuses primarily on environmental and natural-resource issues. It emphasizes the advantages of free markets and the importance of private property rights in environmental protection. PERC's publications include the monthly *PERC Reports* and papers in the PERC Policy Series such as "Population Growth, Economic Freedom, and the Rule of Law" and "The National Forests: For Whom and for What?"

Rainforest Action Network (RAN)
221 Pine St., Suite 500
  San Francisco, CA 94104
(415) 398-4404 • fax: (415) 398-2732
e-mail: rainforest@ran.org
Web site: www.ran.org

RAN works to preserve the world's rain forests through activism by addressing the logging of tropical timber, cattle ranching in rain forests, and the rights of indigenous rain forest peoples. It also seeks to educate the public about the environmental effects of tropical hardwood logging. RAN's publications include the monthly *Action Report* and the semiannual *World Rainforest Report*.

Sierra Club
85 Second St., 2nd Fl., San Francisco, CA 94105-3441
(415) 977-5500 • fax: (415) 977-5799
e-mail: information@sierraclub.org
Web site: www.sierraclub.org

The Sierra Club is a nonprofit public interest organization that promotes conservation of the natural environment by influencing public policy decisions—legislative, administrative, legal, and electoral. It publishes *Sierra* magazine as well as books on the environment.

Union of Concerned Scientists (UCS)
2 Brattle Square
 Cambridge, MA 02238-9105
(617) 547-5552 • fax: (617) 864-9405
e-mail: ucs@ucsusa.org
Web site: www.ucsusa.org

UCS aims to advance responsible public policy in areas where science and technology play important roles. Its programs emphasize transportation reform, arms control, safe and renewable energy technologies, and sustainable agriculture. UCS publications include the twice-yearly magazine *Catalyst,* the quarterly newsletter *Earthwise,* and the reports "Greener SUVs" and "Greenhouse Crisis: The American Response."

U.S. Environmental Protection Agency (EPA)
Ariel Ross Bldg., 1200 Pennsylvania Ave. NW
 Washington, DC 20460
(202) 272-0167
Web Site: www.epa.gov

The EPA is the government agency charged with protecting human health and safeguarding the natural environment. It works to protect Americans from environmental health risks, to enforce federal environmental regulations, and to ensure that environmental protection is an integral consideration in U.S. policy. The EPA publishes many reports, fact sheets, and educational materials.

U.S. Fish and Wildlife Service
1849 C St. NW, Washington, DC 20242
(800) 344-9453
Web site: www.fws.gov

The U.S. Fish and Wildlife Service is a network of regional offices, national wildlife refuges, research and development centers, national fish hatcheries, and wildlife law enforcement agents. The service's primary goal is to conserve, protect, and enhance fish and wildlife and their habitats. It publishes an endangered species list as well as fact sheets, pamphlets, and information on the Endangered Species Act.

Worldwatch Institute
1776 Massachusetts Ave. NW
  Washington, DC 20036-1904
(202) 452-1999 • fax: (202) 296-7365
e-mail: worldwatch@worldwatch.org
Web site: www.worldwatch.org

Worldwatch is a research organization that analyzes and calls attention to global problems, including environmental concerns such as the loss of cropland, forests, habitat, species, and water supplies. It compiles the annual *State of the World* and *Vital Signs* anthologies and publishes the bimonthly *World Watch* magazine.

Bibliography

Books

Curtis D. Anderson and Judy Anderson

Electric and Hybrid Cars: A History. Jefferson, NC: McFarland, 2004.

Keith Bradsher

High and Mighty: The Dangerous Rise of the SUV. New York: PublicAffairs, 2004.

Richard Brewer

Conservancy: The Land Trust Movement in America. Hanover, NH: University Press of New England, 2001.

Bonnie B. Burgess

Fate of the Wild: The Endangered Species Act and the Future of Biodiversity. Athens: University of Georgia Press, 2003.

Robert S. Devine

Bush Versus the Environment. New York: Anchor, 2004.

John S. Dryzek

The Politics of the Earth: Environmental Discourse. Oxford, UK: Oxford University Press, 2005.

Andres R. Edwards

The Sustainability Revolution: Portrait of a Paradigm Shift. Gabriola Island, BC, Canada: New Society, 2005.

Eric T. Freyfogle

The Land We Share: Private Property and the Common Good. Washington, DC: Shearwater Books, 2003.

Ross Gelbspan

Boiling Point: How Politicians, Big Oil and Coal, Journalists and Activists Are

Fueling the Climate Crisis—and What We Can Do to Avert Disaster. New York: Basic Books, 2004.

Francis Harris, ed. *Global Environmental Issues.* New York: Wiley, 2004.

Robert Higgs and Carl P. Close *Re-Thinking Green: Alternatives to Environmental Bureaucracy.* Oakland, CA: Independent Institute, 2004.

Peter Hoffman *Tomorrow's Energy: Hydrogen, Fuel Cells, and the Prospects for a Cleaner Planet.* Cambridge, MA: MIT Press, 2002.

Peter Huber *Hard Green: Saving the Environment from Environmentalists.* New York: Basic Books, 2000.

Robert F. Kennedy Jr. *Corporate Crimes Against Nature.* New York: HarperCollins, 2004.

Bjorn Lomborg *The Skeptical Environmentalist: Measuring the Real State of the World.* Cambridge, UK: Cambridge University Press, 2001.

Mark Lynas *High Tide: The Truth About Our Climate Crisis.* New York: Picador, 2004.

Patrick J. Michaels *Meltdown: The Predictable Distortion of Global Warming by Scientists, Politicians, and the Media.* Washington, DC: Cato Institute, 2005.

Jim Motavalli, ed. *Feeling the Heat: Dispatches from the Frontlines of Climate Change.* New York: Routledge, 2004.

Jeremy Rifkin   *The Hydrogen Economy.* New York: Tarcher, 2003.

Aldo V. da Rosa   *Fundamentals of Renewable Energy Processes.* Burlington, MA: Academic Press, 2005.

Carolyn Servid and Hank Lentfer, eds.   *Arctic Refuge: A Circle of Testimony.* Minneapolis: Milkweed Editions, 2001.

James Gustave Speth   *Red Sky at Morning: America and the Crisis of the Global Environment.* New Haven, CT: Yale University Press, 2004.

Norman J. Vig and Michael E. Kraft, eds.   *Environmental Policy: New Directions for the Twenty-First Century.* Washington, DC: CQ Press, 2005.

Periodicals

Kimberly Jordan Allen   "Edible History: Discovering the Benefits of Heirloom Fruits and Vegetables," *E: The Environmental Magazine,* May/June 2005.

David Bellamy   "Global Warming? What a Load of Poppycock!" *London Daily Mail,* July 9, 2004.

Lester R. Brown   "Rescuing a Planet Under Stress," *Humanist,* November/December 2003.

H. Sterling Burnett   "Global Warming: Religion or Science?" *Human Events,* July 27, 2005.

Ross Clark — "What's Good for GM Is Good for the World," *Spectator*, October 25, 2003.

Alexander Cockburn — "Hot Air Is Bad for Us," *Nation*, September 3, 2001.

Jerry Flint — "The Holy War on SUVs," *Forbes Global*, March 3, 2003.

Karen Garrison — "Extinction of Ocean Fish: A Growing Threat," *Endangered Species Update*, September/October 2002.

Ellen Goodman — "Environmentalism Endangered," *Liberal Opinion Week*, September 15, 2003.

William Norman Grigg — "Hijacking Spaceship Earth," *New American*, August 12, 2002.

Jenny Hogan and Philip Cohen — "Is the Green Dream Doomed to Fail? Without Real Commitment and Substantial Subsidies Renewable Energy Sources Will Never Replace Fossil Fuel," *New Scientist*, July 17, 2004.

Corinna Kester — "Diesels Versus Hybrids: Comparing the Environmental Costs," *World Watch*, July/August 2005.

David R. Legates — "Global Warming Smear Targets," *Washington Times*, August 26, 2003.

Jason Leopold — "Opening the Arctic to Development," *Z Magazine*, June 2005.

Bill McKibben — "Driving Global Warming," *Christian Century*, May 16, 2001.

Bill McKibben "A Special Report on Global Warming, Big Money, Junk Science, and the Climate of Denial," *Mother Jones*, May/June 2005.

Martin Miller "Three Decades of Recovery," *Endangered Species Update*, April–June 2004.

Marc Morano "Enviros 'Ticket' SUVs," *NewsMax*, September 2003.

Robert Paehlke "Greenville: Applying Green Principles to Buildings and Urban Planning Is a Sound Long-Term Investment of Public Dollars," *Alternatives Journal*, November/December 2004.

Burton Richter "Reconciling Global Warming and Increasing Energy Demand," *Journal of Business Administration and Policy Analysis*, Annual 2002.

Roddy Scheer "Ocean Rescue: Can We Head Off a Marine Cataclysm?" *E: The Environmental Magazine*, July/August 2005.

Kathryn Schulz "Global Warming Right Now," *Rolling Stone*, February 20, 2003.

Daniel R. immons and Randy T. Simmons "The Endangered Species Act Turns 30," *Regulation*, Winter 2003.

Roy Spencer "Global Warming: Technology to the Rescue," *Pipeline and Gas Journal*, August 2005.

Andrew Stephen "America Produces 23 Percent of the World's Carbon Dioxide, and the Glaciers in Montana National Park Are Melting," *New Statesman*, September 8, 2003.

Jerry Taylor "Sustainable Development, a Dubious Solution in Search of a Problem," *Cato Institute Policy Analysis*, August 26, 2002.

Donovan Webster and Michael Scherer "No Clear Skies," *Mother Jones*, September/October 2003.

Jennifer Weeks "Code Blue: Mobilizing to Save the Oceans," *E: The Environmental Magazine*, November/December 2004.

David Whitman "Partly Sunny: Why Enviros Can't Admit That Bush's Clear Skies Initiative Isn't Half Bad," *Washington Monthly*, December 2004.

George Will "Environmentalists Encourage Doomsday Thinking," *Conservative Chronicle*, December 4, 2002.

Carl Zimmer "Zeroing in on Climate Change," *Newsweek International*, December 1, 2003.

Index